CLEARING THE PATH FOR DEVELOPING LEARNERS

Essential Literacy Skills to Support Achievement in Every Content Area

PEG GRAFWALLNER

Solution Tree | Press

555 North Morton Street
Bloomington, IN 47404
800.733.6786 (toll free) / 812.336.7700
FAX: 812.336.7790

email: info@SolutionTree.com
SolutionTree.com

Visit **go.SolutionTree.com/literacy** to download the free reproducibles in this book.

Printed in the United States of America

Library of Congress Cataloging-in-Publication Data

Names: Grafwallner, Peggy J., 1960- author.

Title: Clearing the path for developing learners : essential literacy skills to support achievement in every content area / Peg Grafwallner.

Description: Bloomington, IN : Solution Tree Press, 2023. | Includes bibliographical references and index.

Identifiers: LCCN 2022056337 (print) | LCCN 2022056338 (ebook) | ISBN 9781954631793 (paperback) | ISBN 9781954631809 (ebook)

Subjects: LCSH: Reading (Secondary) | Reading comprehension. | Language arts--Correlation with content subjects. | Reading disability. | Response to internvention (Learning disabled children)

Classification: LCC LB1632 .G73 2023 (print) | LCC LB1632 (ebook) | DDC 428.4071/2--dc23/eng/20230126

LC record available at https://lccn.loc.gov/2022056337

LC ebook record available at https://lccn.loc.gov/2022056338

Solution Tree
Jeffrey C. Jones, CEO
Edmund M. Ackerman, President

Solution Tree Press
President and Publisher: Douglas M. Rife
Associate Publishers: Todd Brakke and Kendra Slayton
Editorial Director: Laurel Hecker
Art Director: Rian Anderson
Copy Chief: Jessi Finn
Production Editor: Paige Duke
Proofreader: Sarah Ludwig
Text and Cover Designer: Kelsey Hoover
Acquisitions Editor: Hilary Goff
Assistant Acquisitions Editor: Elijah Oates
Content Development Specialist: Amy Rubenstein
Associate Editor: Sarah Ludwig
Editorial Assistant: Anne Marie Watkins

ACKNOWLEDGMENTS

Solution Tree Press would like to thank the following reviewers:

Gina Cherkowski
Educational Researcher
Calgary, Alberta, Canada

Nathalie Fournier
French Immersion Teacher
Prairie South School Division
Moose Jaw, Saskatchewan, Canada

Kelly Hilliard
Math Teacher
McQueen High School
Reno, Nevada

Erin Kruckenberg
Fifth-Grade Teacher
Harvard Community Unit School District 50
Harvard, Illinois

Shanna Martin
Middle School Teacher & Instructional Coach
School District of Lomira
Lomira, Wisconsin

Visit **go.SolutionTree.com/literacy** to download the free reproducibles in this book.

TABLE OF CONTENTS

Reproducibles are in italics.

ABOUT THE AUTHOR

Peg Grafwallner, MEd, is an instructional coach and reading specialist at Ronald W. Reagan High School, an urban International Baccalaureate school located on the south side of Milwaukee, Wisconsin. Peg has more than thirty years of experience in education. She began her career as an English teacher at a private high school and eventually became an alternative education teacher in a suburban district. She has taught graduate-level courses on reading and writing in the content areas, with an emphasis on differentiation and interventions. She now supports teachers in seamlessly embedding literacy without disrupting their classroom objectives. Peg models how to create comprehensive literacy lessons meant to enhance skill building as she coaches and assists teachers in creating these lessons.

Peg is a member of the Wisconsin State Reading Association (WSRA), the Wisconsin Council of Teachers of English (WCTE), the National Council of Teachers of English (NCTE), and ASCD. As the parent of a gifted and talented son and a daughter who once received special education, Peg offers a unique educational lens that focuses on supporting students of all abilities in realizing their potential in the classroom and beyond. She is a blogger, author, and national presenter whose topics include coaching, engagement, and inclusion. Her articles have appeared in *The Missouri Reader*, *Exceptional Parent*, the *WSRA Journal*, and the *Illinois Reading Council Journal*. She has written for several websites and blogs, including Edutopia, *ASCD Inservice*, Education Week's *Classroom Q&A With Larry Ferlazzo*, KQED's *In the Classroom*, and *Literacy and NCTE*. She has also appeared on numerous podcasts, such as *Cult of Pedagogy*, *BAM! Radio*, *Anchored in Education*, *Easy EdTech*, and *Ed: Conversations About the Teaching Life*. Peg is also the author of *Lessons Learned From the Special Education Classroom: Creating Opportunities for All Students to Listen, Learn, and Lead*; *Ready to Learn: The FRAME Model for Optimizing Student Success*; and *Not Yet . . . And That's OK: How Productive Struggle Fosters Student Learning*.

Peg has a bachelor's degree in English and a mentoring certification from Cardinal Stritch University, a master's degree in curriculum and instruction and an alternative education certification from Marian University, and a reading specialist certification from the University of Wisconsin–Milwaukee.

To book Peg Grafwallner for professional development, contact pd@SolutionTree.com.

INTRODUCTION

"Every teacher must be a teacher of literacy."

In the early years of my career, I cringed every time I heard someone say these words. As a certified English teacher and a certified reading specialist, I felt that statement oversimplified what it meant to teach literacy; after all, I specifically earned licensures in areas that focused on research, resources, skills, and strategies that added to my expertise. I designed differentiated and scaffolded lessons and collaborated with teachers to implement the practices in their classrooms. I possessed a specific skill set targeted to teaching literacy. I would never assume myself to be a teacher of mathematics or science or world languages; conversely, I wouldn't expect a classroom teacher to assume the role of literacy specialist. However, that changed as I saw how students' poor grasp of essential skills presents a significant educational barrier to their success in the classroom. Students who haven't yet mastered essential reading and writing skills struggle to engage with grade-level content in their courses.

As an instructional coach and reading specialist, I work with teachers across content areas to embed essential literacy skills into their classroom objectives. While essential literacy skills are foundational in humanities classes, perhaps they are not as explicit in an art class, a music class, or a physical education class. Therefore, I work with teachers in all disciplines to ensure that essential literacy skills are explicit in their lessons. My goal is not to add more to a teacher's plate; rather, I offer tools and practices for embedding essential literacy skills into what a teacher is already doing. In this way, teachers develop an essential literacy skills toolbox.

As a result of my experience with teachers and students in K–12 classrooms, I'm convinced that *every* teacher must embed essential literacy skills into their classroom.

This is the surest way to clear students' path to success of obstacles that prevent them from engaging with their learning. This book will show you how.

In the remainder of this introduction, I share why students need all teachers to teach essential literacy skills. I provide a basic definition of essential skills as well as a list of which literacy skills are included. I also discuss how to embed essential skills in your classroom. Finally, I offer an overview of how the rest of the book will unfold.

Becoming an Essential Literacy Skills Teacher

My thinking around the teaching of essential literacy skills (which I'll refer to simply as *essential skills* going forward) has changed for three key reasons: (1) many students lack these skills; (2) without them, a student is unable to comprehend texts; and (3) without comprehension, a student is unable to communicate as a mathematician, historian, artist, analyst, or other chosen professional role. Let's look at each of these issues in more detail.

Students are leaving school and entering the workforce underequipped with literacy and numeracy skills. Labor economists Neeta Fogg, Paul Harrington, and Ishwar Khatiwada (2019) authored a report analyzing skills and earnings in the full-time labor force, uncovering troubling trends among professionals. Consider the following from the preface to their report:

> There are large groups of college graduates who lose out on the seemingly automatic earnings premium from their degree, and . . . their failure is related to a lack of skills. One of every five bachelor's degree holders among employed college graduates ages 21 to 65 lacks some important skills in literacy. For numeracy, the number is one in three. (Fogg et al., 2019, p. 1)

Imagine all the ways you rely on basic literacy and numeracy skills to thrive in your vocation. Now imagine struggling with those everyday tasks because you lack the necessary competencies *despite* your status as a college graduate. This is the reality Fogg, Harrington, and Khatiwada (2019) describe, along with the resulting loss of earnings. What happened to those graduates during their K–12 education?

K–12 students who don't master essential literacy skills are unable to comprehend texts. Without comprehension, they fall behind—not just in language arts courses but in *all* academic areas. According to Matthew Lynch (2020) from The Edvocate:

> Many students struggle with reading comprehension, and this can put a serious strain on a child throughout all classroom subjects. Because learning all academic content requires reading in some form, students who struggle with reading comprehension often fall far behind their classmates academically in multiple areas.

Students who fall behind their peers experience additional challenges with motivation and engagement as they question their ability to achieve. It's not unusual to see students engage in "rude behaviors because they have become disengaged from the class" (Eberly Center, n.d.a). These students often become frustrated and apathetic toward learning, thus beginning a spiral that can be challenging to end.

Finally, when students feel frustrated or apathetic due to their poor literacy skills, they are unable to see themselves as mathematicians, historians, artists, analysts, or other professionals in their chosen field. This skill set is essential for all students to thrive on their chosen career path. "Literacy and numeracy are prerequisites for almost all higher order competencies; these foundational skills are necessary for [students] to . . . fully participate in society and the workplace as adults," write research fellows Carmen Belafi, Yue-Yi Hwa, and Michelle Kaffenberger (2020, p. 1). When students have the capacity to fully participate in society, they are able to make worthwhile and meaningful choices that add value to not only their quality of life but also their community.

The solution? Belafi, Hwa, and Kaffenberger (2020) call for educators, policymakers, and authorities to prioritize universal, early, conceptual, and procedural mastery of essential skills. That is precisely the aim of this book: to inspire and equip all teachers to teach essential skills in the classroom so they clear the path for students to achieve at high levels during their K–12 education and beyond.

Defining Essential Skills

What are essential skills, and which skills are included? *Essential skills* are those that allow students to develop basic literacy, numeracy, and transferable skills. They are the fundamental competencies that students require to build lives of learning. You'll notice that numeracy is part of the essential skills definition. However, the scope of this book focuses exclusively on essential literacy skills due to my experience and expertise in the field of literacy.

For the purposes of this book, I've identified the following seven essential skills that all students need to be successful in the classroom and their chosen career. This list resulted from a process of unpacking state academic standards my team and I completed in hopes of boosting ACT scores, a process I cover in more detail in chapter 3 (page 31).

1. Locate the main idea and identify supporting details.
2. Compose a summary.
3. Interpret and apply academic vocabulary.
4. Identify and apply inference.
5. Identify and understand cause–effect relationships.
6. Identify and understand relationships using compare and contrast.
7. Delineate and evaluate arguments.

As you can see from this list, teaching essential skills is not about teaching students to decode, and thus, to read. This book *is not* a guide to teaching such foundational literacy skills as phonemic awareness, phonics, and sight words. This book *is* a guide to creating a toolbox of essential skill-building strategies teachers can customize and apply to their particular grade level and content area to support literacy. It's about learning to build your instruction around essential skills. Students need daily repeated practice working with essential skills in order to apply and transfer their learning in the classroom. Teachers need to practice teaching essential skills daily if they hope to remove the educational barriers students are facing. In addition, the timely benefit to both students and teachers of embedding essential skills in the classroom is a proactive approach to intervention.

Embedding Essential Skills as a Proactive Approach to Intervention

You might be thinking, "How can I explicitly incorporate essential skills into my daily teaching without disrupting the content?" Incorporating essential skills doesn't mean scrapping all the hard work teachers put into designing lessons and gathering resources. As an instructional coach, I understand the time and effort teachers invest in gathering videos, primary and secondary documents, guest speakers, research-based articles, and other resources to make their lessons real, relevant, and relatable to students. When I collaborate with classroom teachers, I see their relationship to the content is primary and essential skill building is secondary. Teachers often have their resources and activities ready to go, but they haven't clearly identified the skills with which to teach those resources and activities during grade- or course-level instruction. I understand this tendency, especially in a public education system where teachers face pressure from administration as well as national and local policies to impart an enormous amount of information and prepare students to achieve at high levels on benchmarks and tests.

Unfortunately, when the explicit teaching of essential skills is missing from these carefully curated lessons, many students who need support with these skills are not able to engage with grade-level and course content in the way teachers expect. When this happens, students cannot actively participate in the lessons. Those skills are the mechanism that empowers students to be the robust learners teachers want them to be.

At this point, sharp-eyed readers might be thinking, "Isn't support for missing essential skills the purpose of intervention?" This is true, but not the full story. There are a variety of approaches to intervention and even more varieties of actual implementation based on factors such as school size, availability of staff, and so on, but let's consider one of the more popular approaches—response to intervention (RTI). Created in 2004, RTI supports schools in identifying students who need extra learning opportunities and providing them with appropriate instructional interventions. As detailed in *Taking Action: A Handbook for RTI at Work*™ (Buffum, Mattos, & Malone, 2018), RTI is delivered in three instructional tiers as illustrated in figure I.1 (page 6).

Although this illustration is predicated on the presence of educators working in collaborative teams, it effectively illustrates the purpose of each tier, the organization of responsibilities at the school and teacher levels, and the scope of impact. Effectively, all grade- and course-level instruction is Tier 1, and it's vital that *all* students have access to this instruction at all times. Tier 2 interventions provide targeted support for students who need to better develop specific skills; these interventions are usually given by teachers in the classroom. Tier 3 most often involves dedicated specialists or intervention teams who provide intensive remediation only for those students most in need at Tier 3. The goal is that as the intervention tier increases, the number of students requiring access to that tier decreases, which is why the pyramid is inverted.

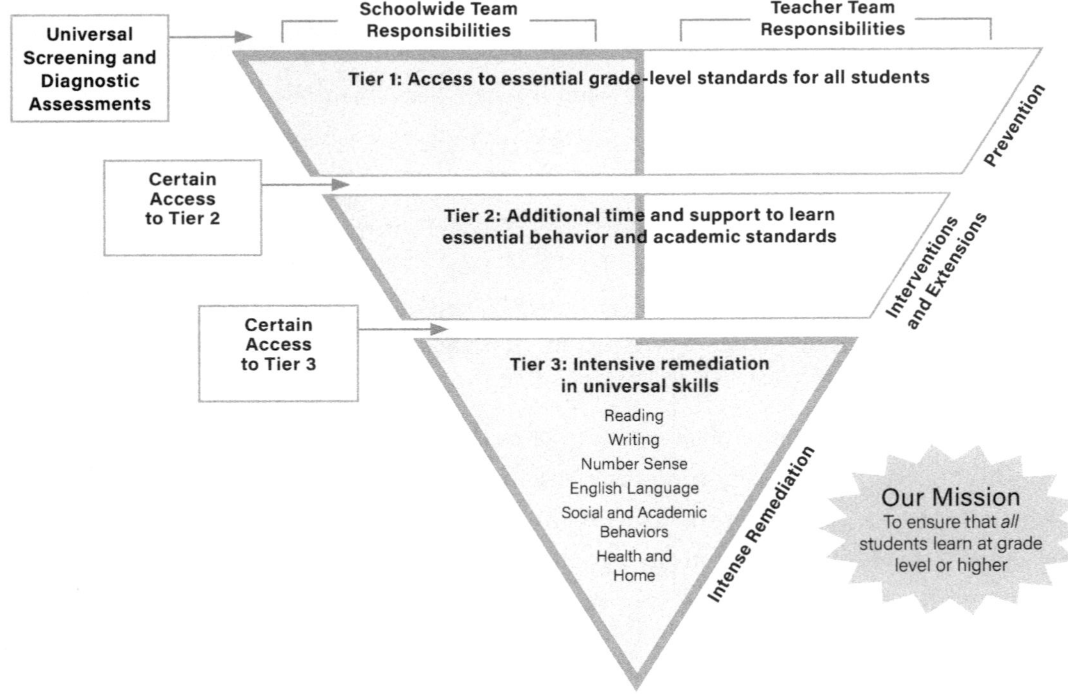

Source: Buffum et al., 2018, p. 18.

FIGURE I.1: The RTI at Work pyramid.

Our goal as educators is to catch students *before* they need interventions—to build up their essential skills toolbox so they are able to critically read, write, and think. According to RTI experts Matthew K. Burns, Rebecca Sarlo, and Hollie Pettersson (n.d.), "Instead of an intervention-focused approach to meeting students' needs, effective programming focuses on prevention, beginning with the intensification of core instruction." Essential skill building is certainly part of this prevention, but it's not the only impact. You will always have students who need dedicated interventions. But when teachers can reinforce those interventions by explicitly implementing essential and cross-curricular skills as part of core grade- and course-level instruction (Tier 1), it can only help accelerate student learning, ensuring all students reap the benefits of a high-quality educational program.

To that end, all teachers are responsible for supporting students to practice and master essential skills along their academic journey. Education scholars Alicia Herbert, Jaime Saavedra, Leanna Marr, and Robert Jenkins (2021) note that essential skills (they refer to them as *foundational*) are "the building blocks for a life of learning. Just as we would not build a house without solid foundations, we cannot expect a child to thrive without solid foundational skills." Students rely on literacy skills to successfully comprehend complex texts in school and beyond. They must have multiple ongoing opportunities to master those critical skills in order to use them effectively and efficiently to become powerful and autonomous learners.

Using the strategies in this book, you'll learn to create explicit time and space in your lessons to teach essential skills within the content, resources, and activities you're already using. This approach maximizes teachers' efforts and supports students in the daily repeated practice of essential skills leading to increased comprehension. Implement essential skill building in all your lessons, and students will have the opportunity to become deliberate readers, writers, and critical thinkers.

Outlining This Book

This book is structured in two parts. Consider part 1 your road map to creating a skill-centered classroom. Part 1 aims to show that reorienting learning around foundational skills is a process, one that teachers achieve with practice over time.

In chapter 1, you learn how to prioritize essential skills in your classroom. You encounter actionable advice for building lessons around essential skills so that students can learn the skills and transfer them to diverse contexts.

In chapter 2, you understand that fostering a supportive classroom culture is key to sustaining skill-centered instruction over the long term. You encounter three areas of focus for this work: (1) embracing productive struggle, (2) establishing scaffolding strategies, and (3) ensuring student engagement.

In chapter 3, you discover how to unpack your state's or province's academic standards to identify the essential skills that are key for your campus and classroom. I describe the process I used to identify the seven skills highlighted in this book and outline a template you can use to design your own process to unpack academic standards.

In chapter 4, you learn how to harness brain-friendly teaching techniques to support students to move toward automaticity with essential skills, which helps them successfully engage with grade- and course-level instruction.

Part 2 is your essential skills starter kit. There, you find seven chapters, each devoted to one of the essential skills.

- Chapter 5 covers foundational skill 1: locate the main idea and identify supporting details.
- Chapter 6 covers foundational skill 2: compose a summary.

- Chapter 7 covers foundational skill 3: interpret and apply academic vocabulary.
- Chapter 8 covers foundational skill 4: identify and apply inference.
- Chapter 9 covers foundational skill 5: identify and understand cause–effect relationships.
- Chapter 10 covers foundational skill 6: identify and understand relationships using compare and contrast.
- Chapter 11 covers foundational skill 7: delineate and evaluate arguments.

Each of these chapters provides a brief overview of the skill, two activities built around that skill, two variations on that activity, and a classroom example of what that might look like. The activities and variations are intentionally basic, written in a way that you can easily customize to your classroom. In this part's chapters, you also find lesson-planning tools, graphic organizers, charts, worksheets, and reproducibles tailored to each skill.

In closing, essential literacy skills support students of all abilities to make sense of text. Without these skills, students fall behind and struggle to reach their full potential in the classroom and their chosen career. It's our responsibility and privilege as teachers to do whatever we can to provide students with those essential skills so they have the tools they need to thrive.

While you may engage with parts of this book in isolation, I recommend using the first three essential skills in order: locate the main idea and identify supporting details, compose a summary, and interpret and apply academic vocabulary. In doing so, you will lay a strong foundation for students. You may use the remaining skills in the order you determine. As you begin explicitly teaching essential skills, you'll start noticing how several skills work synergistically within a single lesson. Essential skills give students the tools they need to be successful—let that success start *now*!

PART 1

YOUR ROAD MAP TO TEACHING ESSENTIAL SKILLS

CHAPTER 1

PRIORITIZE ESSENTIAL SKILLS IN YOUR CLASSROOM

In the introduction (page 1), you learned that many students leave school without achieving mastery of essential literacy skills. I briefly touched on Fogg and colleagues' (2019) research illustrating that college graduates enter the workforce with inadequate literacy skills. But what is happening with teachers and their students in K–12 classrooms that leads graduates to these outcomes?

Students are in the midst of a learning crisis. The Population Council's Nicole Haberland and Timothy Abuya (2021) write:

> For decades, the global education system has not been educating the majority of its children adequately, largely because we have failed to connect how policies and programs can leverage data and evidence to reduce inequalities and get all children in school and learning.

Some areas of the globe experience this crisis more keenly than others. But beginning in 2020, the global COVID-19 pandemic escalated the effects so that every school, every teacher, and every classroom has been touched by learning loss. Haberland and Abuya (2021) go on to say:

> The COVID-19 pandemic is amplifying this crisis. While the full educational repercussions of the pandemic are just beginning to unfold, an additional eleven million primary and secondary students are projected to drop out of school due to COVID-19. . . . Children need to get back to school and build back their literacy and numeracy skills.

A March 2022 UNICEF report finds that "even before the pandemic hit, the majority of children in countries analyzed had not mastered foundational skills in either reading or numeracy by the time they reached Grade 3" (United Nations Children's Fund, 2022, p. 1). Learning loss only compounds over time. Imagine what these circumstances mean for the global education system. A large number of students entered middle school and high school without mastery of essential skills *before* the pandemic. Given the personal and academic upheaval students have faced since the onset of the pandemic, the lack of opportunity to practice and master essential skills is a significant educational barrier to K–12 students. It's no wonder graduates are struggling with their professional roles and responsibilities.

Every teacher must make skill building an explicit, repeated feature of daily instruction in order to equip students to master essential skills, apply them to diverse contexts, and remove the educational barriers students face at Tiers 2 and 3. In this chapter, we'll discuss embedding essential skills in instruction by showing you how to practice building lessons around essential skills rather than prioritizing an activity and allowing the skill to be an afterthought. As you become accustomed to centering skills in instruction, you will need to ensure that students also have ample opportunity to practice transferring essential skills to new contexts. By witnessing students move to application and transfer of these skills, you will know that students are approaching mastery of skills.

Embedding Essential Skills in Instruction

Regardless of whether you wish to support students in mastering essential skills by grade 3 or to help them recover from learning loss and work toward mastery during secondary years, the need is the same. Students at all levels need opportunities to practice essential skills on a regular basis. Therefore, all teachers need strategies that enable them to embed these skills into instruction, in all content areas, all year long. Introducing a skill, teaching it, practicing it a few times, and moving on to the next one is not sufficient to overcome the educational barriers students face. In the following paragraphs, we'll explore three keys to embedding essential skills into your lessons: (1) introduce one skill at a time, (2) build your lessons around essential skills, and (3) practice transferring essential skills.

Introduce One Skill at a Time

Students need explicit instruction and frequent practice with one skill at a time in order to master essential skills. Monitor students' progress as they practice to ensure they're moving toward mastery. According to the Eberly Center (n.d.b) at Carnegie Mellon University, teachers must "give students more practice at developing fluency of basic skills." When students achieve *fluency*—meaning they are able to use new skills automatically—they can move seamlessly from one skill to another.

In addition, students need opportunities to practice through a variety of learning modalities, such as visual, auditory, reading, writing, and kinesthetic. Teachers know that every student learns differently. Therefore, it makes sense that practicing essential skills in a variety of ways helps deepen students' understanding of those skills. If we don't offer students opportunities to practice, they may not develop the ability to transfer their learning. Achieving transfer is essential for students to thrive in diverse contexts. Giving students various ways to learn and ample opportunity to practice offers them academic freedom to be creative in their learning.

Let's look at an example. Eighth-grade social studies teacher Ms. Lin recognizes an opportunity to build a lesson about the Great Depression around the essential skill of identifying and understanding cause–effect relationships. She offers students the following options.

- She asks students to create a chart of the causes and effects of the Great Depression and hangs it up in the classroom so students can refer to it throughout the unit.
- She facilitates a debate about the causes and effects of the Great Depression and records it for future study.
- She instructs students to write a paragraph of causes and a paragraph of effects regarding the Great Depression that students will share with their peers.
- She asks students to create a board game with game pieces, similar to *Monopoly*, where students could "land" on causes; they must then provide the corresponding effects.

Notice the various modalities the students can choose from and the opportunity these create for students to access creative expression. They can design a chart, host a debate, share ideas with peers, create a board game, and more. These ideas inspire students to transfer the essential skill of identifying and understanding cause–effect relationships beyond the status quo expectations of the classroom to an engaging, exciting, and empowering learning experience!

Once you have introduced students to a single skill or series of skills, you can combine two or three as a daily practice of skills. For example, imagine that students have been working through the first three skills—locate the main idea and identify supporting details, compose a summary, and interpret and apply academic vocabulary—and now they're moving on to inference. The teacher gives students an informational article about microplastics and tasks them with underlining the main idea and details and highlighting any unknown vocabulary. Next, the teacher pauses the activity, taking time to explicitly teach students to identify and apply inference—the act of reading between the lines. The teacher reads a passage from the article aloud and models identifying and applying inference, highlighting the relevant text. Students then return to the activity, this time finding another example of inference in the article and sharing it with a partner. As students work on this new skill, they continue to practice the former skills of identifying main idea, supporting details, and vocabulary terms. This will likely happen more automatically now that they are moving toward mastery. Their focus is on practicing the new inference skill.

As teachers "move incrementally from simple tasks to those with extra demands" (Eberly Center, n.d.b), or from teaching a specific skill to practicing several skills, students grasp this challenge because they've received the necessary time to practice each skill.

Build Your Lessons Around Essential Skills

Essential skills should be the cornerstone of a lesson, rather than a secondary element or afterthought. When I collaborate with a student teacher regarding skill building, I sometimes notice the teacher center the learning on an activity rather than skills. In these instances, I explain the critical importance of designing lessons that focus on skills and using the activity as, perhaps, a warm-up for engagement. I write about one such instance in an article for Edutopia:

> Although engaging students in their learning is certainly necessary, the student teacher I was working with became acutely aware of the value of the skills she was attempting to help students develop and why those skills—not the activity—should drive instruction. (Grafwallner, 2019)

Teachers unaccustomed to working with essential skills in this way may at first find it challenging to shift their practice. Think about the workshops or presentations you've attended and how excited you've been to bring something back to share with your students. Have you ever thought, "I can't wait to use this on Monday morning"? What were you sharing? Was it an essential skill or an activity? It was likely an activity—the vehicle for teaching that essential content. *How* you teach the content is flexible. *What* you're teaching is not. Our task as teachers is to ensure that we're not so caught up on how we're teaching that we fail to center the essential skill, the what. Consider the following tips to help you reorient your lesson planning around essential skills.

- Identify which skill or skills will serve as the cornerstone of your lesson. Remember to introduce a new skill before combining it with others.
- Explicitly name and demonstrate the skill (providing a definition and context if needed): "Today, we will use the skill of inference to read this particular text and determine various conclusions based on evidence from the text."
- Embed it into the content so students see how the skill can be applied.
- Discuss potential opportunities students might encounter to transfer the skill to another situation. When you see students successfully transferring the skill, celebrate the win!

Give students the opportunity to practice that skill in another way. If you taught the skill through an informational article, consider giving students the chance to practice with alternative modalities to promote transfer.

Part 2 (page 49) of this book provides examples and resources you can use to craft lesson plans that use essential skills as the cornerstone of lessons.

Practice Transferring Essential Skills

How will teachers know that students are moving toward mastery? *Transfer.* "'Transfer' is a cognitive practice whereby a learner's mastery of knowledge or skills in one context enables them to apply that knowledge or skill in a different context" (Poorvu Center for Teaching and Learning, n.d.). We see transfer when students are able to take something they have learned and apply it in another context.

As an example, imagine that I have taught my anatomy students to identify and understand cause–effect relationships. Now, for practice (and for fun), I ask students to watch their favorite TV show after school and see if they can pick out any cause–effect examples and be ready to share them with the class the next day. Essential skills aren't just useful in the classroom—they're part of everyday interactions with the world.

That's the point! Encourage students to explicitly notice how and when they draw on those skills in their everyday lives. Most importantly, encourage students to share with peers how they have used those skills in various situations and experiences.

Teachers must provide repeated opportunities for students to apply and transfer the essential skills they're learning. Special education teacher Nina Parrish (2022) explains, "Students benefit from trying multiple ways to learn and practice a specific skill so that they can discover what works best for them in different contexts." As teachers see students succeeding at these higher-level tasks, they'll know students are approaching mastery.

When you offer students time in class to practice essential skills, make sure those opportunities are purposeful and embedded within the content. This is not about repetition or memorization but about creation of a learning environment with organic and frequent opportunities for students to apply and transfer the essential skills they're learning. Researchers Mary Brabeck, Jill Jeffrey, and Sara Fry (2015) explain:

> Deliberate practice is not the same as rote repetition. Rote repetition—simply repeating a task—will not by itself improve performance. Deliberate practice involves attention, rehearsal and repetition and leads to new knowledge or skills that can later be developed into more complex knowledge and skills.

Let's look at an example. Mr. Martin gives students a page of complex text about why food insecurity is on the rise. Now that the students have been practicing how to identify and apply inference for the last month during their study of nutrition, he is curious to see how they will apply their skills to this new context. As Mr. Martin reviews the students' work later that week, he is encouraged to see the diverse ways students applied their essential skills in engaging with the activity. He notices the following choices in the students' work.

- Students used academic vocabulary resources to define the challenging vocabulary in the text.
- Students highlighted the text to identify the main idea and subsequent details.
- Students made notations in the margin sharing their inferences garnered from the reading.

Seeing students' diverse use of essential skills and their high-level engagement with the text, Mr. Martin confirms that students are mastering the essential skills and successfully applying and transferring them to new contexts.

This example presents a best-case scenario, right? Everything worked out perfectly. Whew! Life in the classroom is rarely this simple, though. What might it look like to anticipate that some students will show proficiency while others will still need support to achieve it? Let's try the example again and notice a few key changes the teacher makes.

Mr. Martin presents students with three texts about why food insecurity is on the rise: (1) a news article from CNN, "Fewer Children Faced Food Insecurity Last Year, but More Elderly Americans Did" (Luhby, 2022); (2) a scholarly article from *Nutrition Journal*, "Food Insecurity Among Households With Children During the COVID-19 Pandemic: Results From a Study Among Social Media Users Across the United States" (Parekh et al., 2021); and (3) an article from *Teen Vogue*, "Food Insecurity and COVID-19: The Fight to Feed America" (Srikrishna, 2021). Students choose which article they will work with for this activity. Mr. Martin instructs students to work with a partner who chose the same article.

Now that students have been practicing how to identify and apply inference for the last month during their study of nutrition, Mr. Martin is curious to see how they will apply their skills to this new context. He observes students working in pairs; he quietly encourages those who demonstrate fluency and steps in to support those who ask for help.

Consider the differences in the two examples.

- Instead of assigning all students to read the same article of complex text, the teacher offers students three articles on the same topic at different levels of difficulty.
- Students work in pairs rather than independently.
- Rather than looking at students' completed work, the teacher observes students working in real time and offers support to those who need more practice to move to fluency.

Giving students a chance to choose their reading and to work with a partner offers an alternative to students who might need a little extra time and feedback to develop their essential skills. Choosing one's own reading "comes [with] an increase in the amount of reading students actually do" (Jarzabek, 2019) since students have the chance to take ownership. In addition, when students are able to work together, they "have to actively engage their understanding of a concept in order to succeed" (National Society of High School Scholars, 2020). Providing choice, opportunity, and support paves the path for students to achieve mastery of essential skills.

Consider the following tips for equipping students to apply and transfer the essential skills they've learned in class.

- **Design lessons with application and transfer in mind:** Worthwhile and purposeful opportunities to practice allow students to deliberately hone those skills and transfer them to all sorts of learning experiences.
- **Model how to apply essential skills:** Giving students practice to apply essential skills in a real-life scenario shows students the value of essential skills and encourages them to utilize these skills in their own situations and experiences.
- **Facilitate transfer of essential skills:** Creating an interdisciplinary unit employing essential skills in two different content areas demonstrates to students that essential skills apply in all academic areas and are useful in diverse contexts.

What might this look like in practice? As an English teacher, I collaborated with a social studies teacher to create an interdisciplinary lesson. Based on my Edutopia article titled "Keeping Learning Real, Relevant, and Relatable" (Grafwallner, 2017a), we wanted students to "learn about where they live by researching how culture, religion, and traditions have shaped their community and perhaps their lives as well." We wanted students to interview their local government leaders and neighbors to learn more about their community and how it has changed over the years. We designed this lesson with the transference of skills in mind since students would be using these skills in both disciplines.

Within that lesson, we chose a variety of essential skills that we wanted to teach to our students, namely these: composing a summary, interpreting and applying academic vocabulary, and identifying and understanding relationships using compare and contrast. We began our unit by explicitly naming and defining these skills and modeling each one to our students as if we were doing the work ourselves.

Next, we created various assessments that required students to summarize the interviews with their government leaders and neighbors about their community, to utilize academic vocabulary from government officials, and to compare and contrast the changes in culture, religion, or traditions throughout their community. For example, several students mentioned they had learned that their community once had neighborhood block parties or potluck dinners. But these traditions had stopped when the organizers moved away.

An essential part of teaching a foundational skill within a content-specific lesson is to show students how to use that skill in other ways. This primes students' brains to recognize opportunities to transfer the skill to diverse contexts. In addition, citing Susan M. Barnett and Stephen J. Ceci (2002), the Poorvu Center for Teaching and Learning (n.d.) explains, "Because transfer signals that a learner's comprehension allows them to recognize how their knowledge can be relevant and to apply it effectively outside original learning conditions, transfer is often considered a hallmark of true learning."

As students connect one content area with another, they apply their essential skills from one situation to another. As teachers witness students transferring essential skills to new learning opportunities, they can trust that students will achieve automaticity and be able to rely on those essential literacy and numeracy skills in and out of the classroom.

CHAPTER 2

FOSTER A SUSTAINABLE CLASSROOM CULTURE

Building lessons around essential literacy skills and supporting students to move toward mastery of those skills sounds great. But how does that work in a classroom of students with diverse needs, abilities, and learning gaps? Trying to juggle so many moving parts can start to feel like building a house of cards.

Expectations from administration, as well as district, state or provincial, and national leaders, can pack on the pressure. The classroom can easily become an environment where students are rewarded for conforming to expectations rather than supported to thrive as authentic learners. Teachers must create a classroom culture that meets students where they are, normalizes productive struggle as part of the learning process, clarifies learning expectations, and provides a consistent structure of support. Without a supportive culture underpinning essential skills instruction, students become frustrated, struggle to engage, or give up altogether.

In this chapter, you will discover practices teachers can adopt to foster a supportive and sustainable classroom culture. Teachers can begin by embracing productive struggle as a natural part of the learning process, what I call the *not-yet approach* (Grafwallner, 2021). They can also establish learning intentions and success criteria for each lesson to communicate their expectations to students and empower them to monitor their own learning. Finally, I discuss elements teachers can focus on to boost student engagement.

Embracing the Not-Yet Approach

Shifting to skill-centered instruction can be challenging for both students and teachers. To make this shift successful and sustainable, everyone in the learning community must be able to respond to obstacles and setbacks without giving up. In short, they must embrace productive struggle. I write about nurturing a culture of productive struggle in my book *Not Yet . . . And That's OK* (Grafwallner, 2021):

> The challenge for teachers is to create a culture where any failure to learn is simply a common and natural indicator that the learning hasn't happened *yet*. But it will. This is the essence of the not-yet approach. It's about how teachers allow for and even encourage setbacks in the classroom, recontextualizing them for students as a crucial and mandatory part of learning. Teachers who foster a not-yet approach and culture in their classroom do the following.
>
> - Empower students to realize that setbacks and obstacles are a beginning point to learning and not an end point.
> - Normalize encountering and overcoming obstacles so they become part of the learning process as students produce new products (completed classwork, essays, projects, and so on).
> - Contextualize setbacks and obstacles as trial-and-error opportunities that assist students in process-based learning and, ultimately, progress.
> - Model how to graciously accept setbacks and obstacles as part of every student's social-emotional endeavor to better themselves and those around them. (p. 2)

Embracing the not-yet approach allows teachers and students to learn essential skills in a supportive and sustainable way. Students will not master these skills the first time they try. Teachers must model for students how to embrace obstacles as part of the learning process rather than shy away from them. As students do experience setbacks and then receive more practice and more opportunities to transfer those skills, students realize that the not-yet mindset is key to the process of moving to mastery.

I observed a health class during a lesson where the teacher introduced students to inference, offering examples from a health article. As I walked around the class, students jotted down one inference in the margin. The teacher asked students to then work with their elbow partner to find more examples from the article. Most students started working together, but I noticed one pair was very quiet.

“Have you found any examples so far?” I asked.

The pair silently shook their heads. One student spoke up. “This is too hard. It doesn’t make sense.”

The other student put down their pencil and shrugged. “I’ll never get it.”

“Hmm, OK. What is it about inference that doesn’t make sense?” I asked.

“Well, do we just always assume something based on what we’re reading?”

I explained that as readers, we often begin our reading with biases and stereotypes. In addition, as we’re reading, we sometimes overlook clues that might help us prove our inferences or assumptions.

I sat down and looked through the article with the students, asking them to point out a sentence for the three of us to work on together. After they picked one out and read it aloud, I asked, “What can we infer or assume from that sentence, and why? What is it telling us that isn’t made very clear?”

Together, the students examined the sentence, inferred information, and explained why it was an example of inference. In our conversation, I modeled those specific questions again and encouraged the students to find another example. Once they demonstrated their understanding, I stood up to leave. I asked them to continue working together and promised I would stop over again in a few minutes to check on their work.

Instead of giving up or staying silent, these students decided to try the activity even though they weren’t successful the first time. With a little extra help, they persevered. After seeing me model how to find inferences and what language to use, the students felt confident to try again. Sometimes that’s all it takes—modeling a specific technique to get students from “I’ll never get it” to “Let me try again!” Our conversation reminded these students that learning is a process that involves working through productive struggle.

Modeling productive struggle and encouraging students to stick with the process is the teacher’s job. But how can teachers spur students to adopt the not-yet approach for themselves? Once students embrace the mindset, the whole class starts to work in sync. The key to getting students invested in productive struggle is building in supports that empower them to monitor their learning and celebrate their progress.

Establishing Scaffolds

When introducing skill-centered instruction, teachers must make the structure of learning explicit so students can monitor their learning and take ownership of it. I write about this key concept in my Edutopia article "What I've Learned From Special Ed Teachers": "Be prepared to break down a lesson and create pieces of learning. When each piece is explained, modeled, practiced, and applied, the parts fit together solidly to form a whole of understanding" (Grafwallner, 2017b). That whole of understanding is not just *what* students learn but *how* they learn it. When students understand and practice monitoring their own learning, they access tools to support their growth during K–12 and beyond.

In my experience, scaffolding offers a way to achieve this. Researchers Linda Darling-Hammond, Lisa Flook, Channa Cook-Harvey, Brigid Barron, and David Osher (2020) explain that teachers need to "provide carefully designed 'scaffolds' to help students take each step in the learning journey with appropriate assistance." *Scaffolding* refers to "a variety of instructional techniques used to move students progressively toward stronger understanding and, ultimately, greater independence in the learning process" (Glossary of Education Reform, 2015). Scaffolds give students the option of extra support they might need toward greater understanding.

Strong scaffolds support students in learning essential skills, applying them in text, and transferring them from one content area to another. A great way to begin to practice scaffolding when teaching essential skills is to establish learning intentions and success criteria for each lesson. I use these well-known concepts as the backbone of my work with teachers in my capacity as an instructional coach. *Learning intentions* are "the essential goals you want students to achieve in a comprehensive unit," and *success criteria* are "the milestones or learning targets you have determined that will enable students to meet the goals represented in their learning intentions" (Grafwallner, 2021, p. 51). In short, learning intentions and success criteria tell students what they need to know and be able to do; learning intentions help students stay focused and involved, and scaffolded success criteria give students the steps they need to achieve those learning intentions.

You'll notice I use the phrase *scaffolded success criteria* when referring to success criteria. When success criteria are scaffolded in a bulleted list according to difficulty, students can self-assess what they know and are able to do. As an example, if a student realizes that they are stuck on the third bullet in the list of success criteria, they can seek out resources to help them. The student can eliminate the strategies they've already used, ask peers for help, or seek assistance from their teacher. With scaffolded success criteria, the onus is on the students to determine where they are stuck. The students can advocate for themselves and move forward in *their* learning. When students know the task in front of them and what they are to do with the task, they are more apt to take ownership of their learning.

Let's look at an example. Ms. Allen is planning a lesson in which her sixth-grade art class will use proper academic vocabulary to critique a piece of art. She identifies the following learning intention and success criteria at the beginning of the lesson.

Vigorous learning intention: I can define and apply five art terms to critique a peer's work through a written summary.
Scaffolded success criteria: I know I am successful because ▪ I can define five art terms, including the word *critique*. ▪ I can critique a peer's work using the appropriate art terminology. ▪ I can write a summary sharing my critique with a peer for future help. ▪ I can verbally share my critique with a peer to help improve their work.

Notice how the learning intention and success criteria provide a simple structure for teachers to embed essential skills (in this case, applying academic vocabulary) into instruction, offer scaffolds, and allow students to monitor their learning and celebrate their progress. While the teacher is responsible for creating the learning intention and scaffolded success criteria, the student takes responsibility for participating in their learning. When students are able to take ownership, they are empowered and emboldened to be successful.

Part 2 (page 49) includes tools you can use for writing your own learning intentions and success criteria as you begin planning lessons around essential skills for your class. As you get comfortable writing and using learning intentions and scaffolded success criteria, share them with students, invite the students' feedback, and practice working with them as a classroom community.

Ensuring Student Engagement

Nurturing student engagement is key to creating a sustainable classroom culture. How do teachers know when students are engaged in their learning? Education researcher Phillip C. Schlechty (2011) writes that four components indicate student engagement: (1) focused attention, (2) commitment, (3) persistence, and (4) meaning making. While it's easy to recognize disengaged students when you see them, it can be challenging to figure out the reason for their lack of engagement. Teachers can't control factors outside the classroom contributing to disengagement, but they can nurture a classroom environment that excites students to participate. In thirty years of teaching, I have never met a student who doesn't want to read and write well. Students *want* to join in the text discussion; their classmates' curiosity is contagious. But when students can't comprehend the text or they lack the vocabulary or background knowledge to participate in a class discussion, they easily disengage from the lesson.

Pause for a moment. Remember a time when you didn't have the skills you needed to participate in a professional capacity or in a social setting. How did you feel? What behaviors did you rely on to cope in that situation? Let's see what happens when we apply that lens to student disengagement.

According to Reading Rockets (n.d.a), "The effects of falling behind in reading and feeling like a failure can take a large toll on kids. . . . Some begin to act out in class or set low expectations for themselves." Think about how disengaged students present in your classroom. Some students may sit quietly, slumped down and focused inward. You can almost see them silently begging you not to call on them during the lesson. Others may look intently at the page in front of them, refusing to make eye contact with you. Some students chronically talk with their neighbor, joke around, or disrupt the learning in other ways. Students exhibiting these behaviors are often labeled *struggling* or *reluctant*. But what happens when we apply the lens of missing or underdeveloped skills? In this light, we see students who don't intend to cause problems, but who (without even realizing it) attempt to cope with feelings of inadequacy, shame, embarrassment, or fear, or a combination of challenging feelings. Disengagement is one way students communicate they don't have what they need to join in the learning.

The tools in part 2 (page 49) will support students to build missing essential skills and strengthen weak ones, increasing engagement over time. In the meantime, there are three areas on which teachers can focus their efforts to foster a classroom environment that supports student engagement: (1) social-emotional learning (SEL), (2) cultural responsiveness, and (3) movement integration.

Social-Emotional Learning

Social-emotional learning is too complex a topic to cover fully in this chapter. Heck, whole books are devoted to the subject; plus, many teachers already incorporate SEL into their classrooms in some capacity. In creating a culture that encourages students to engage in the learning, though, we can think about SEL in terms of *connection*. When teachers value connection as a tenet of classroom culture, students are more likely to experience safety and belonging. Authors Jason E. Harlacher and Sara A. Whitcomb (2022) write about this in *Bolstering Student Resilience*:

> *Connection* refers to the relation students feel to school, to each other, and to the teacher. This is a critical concept, because students who feel positively connected to at least one adult are more engaged with their schooling and at lower risk for delinquent or risky behavior (Anderson, Christenson, Sinclair, & Lehr, 2004; Decker, Dona, & Christenson, 2007; Zolkoski, 2019). (p. 8)

Building connectedness comes more naturally to some teachers than it does to others, but all teachers can incorporate simple practices into their interactions with students to create meaningful bonds. Consider the following ideas.

- Greet students by name each day as they enter the classroom.
- Take note of students' interests and passions, and engage them in conversation on those topics. This can be as simple as sharing an article, meme, or joke on the subject. When all else fails, try asking students a question about their particular interest, maybe something you're curious about.
- Find genuine ways to compliment students.
- When you notice a student's expertise, invite the student to share it with the class or take on a leadership role where that expertise is valuable.
- Celebrate students' personal and academic wins, successes, and accomplishments as a class.

- Use emotional check-ins to allow students to express their feelings and needs.
- Praise students when they practice connection and belonging with one another.

Which of these do you already practice? What else would you add to this list? Before moving on to the next section, pause for a moment and consider practices you would like to incorporate to encourage student engagement.

Cultural Responsiveness

Like social-emotional learning, cultural responsiveness is a complex topic. Teacher educator and author Zaretta Hammond (2015) writes, "Far from being a bag of tricks, culturally responsive teaching is a pedagogical approach firmly rooted in learning theory and cognitive science" (p. 16). What is culturally responsive teaching, and how does it help students build intellective capacity and more willingly engage in learning? *Culturally responsive teaching* is a pedagogical approach that supports culturally and linguistically diverse students to engage in higher-order thinking and become independent learners.

Hammond (2015) identifies four practice areas of culturally responsive teaching, which are interdependent and most effective when they're done together. "In unison they create a synergetic effect. . . . When the tools and practices are blended together, they create the social, emotional, and cognitive conditions that allow students to more actively engage and take ownership of their learning process" (Hammond, 2015, p. 18).

1. **Awareness:** Teachers develop an awareness of their sociopolitical consciousness. They understand their role in both perpetuating and challenging inequity. They practice becoming aware of and managing their social-emotional responses to diverse and marginalized students.
2. **Learning partnerships:** Teachers understand that the brain is wired for connection and, therefore, focus on building genuine bonds of trust and respect with students across differences.
3. **Information processing:** Teachers use what they know about brain-based learning and students' cultural models to strengthen and expand students' capacity to engage in higher-order learning. They orchestrate instruction to align with students' cultural modes of learning.

4. **Community building:** Teachers create a learning environment in which dependent learners feel socially and intellectually safe to take risks and move toward independence. They understand that the physical environment is not neutral but rather reflective of worldview and culture; therefore, teachers strive to create an environment in which diverse students experience care, support, and belonging.

As you can see, practicing and integrating these four elements requires teachers' dedication and investment. It requires commitment to awareness, understanding, and growth over time. Each teacher's relationship to these practices will be unique. Pause for a moment and reflect on your connection to these four practices. How do you see these at work in your classroom? How would you like to expand your relationship to these practices?

Committing to culturally responsive teaching initiates powerful changes in the classroom environment and in relationships between teachers and students as well as students and their peers. Not only do all students begin to experience belonging in and ownership of their learning, but students from diverse cultures witness what it looks and feels like to respect, value, and celebrate differences.

When cultural responsiveness is a natural part of the classroom experience, students are willing to take risks in their responses, in their work, and in their relationships with others. Because students feel comfortable sharing their diverse identities and cultural expressions, they are willing to be courageous learners in the classroom.

Movement Integration

Students disengage from learning for a variety of reasons, but a common one is their need to take a brain break, get their blood flowing, or move around. Teachers know how it feels to sit still for too long, focus too hard on a single task, or wade through brain fog. Students have these experiences too, and the status quo classroom asks them to sit far longer than their bodies are accustomed to.

In *30+ Movement Strategies to Boost Cognitive Engagement*, educator and author Rebecca Stobaugh (2023) argues that movement in the classroom is a powerful and simple tool teachers can access to boost student engagement. Benefits of movement integration include positive health outcomes, collaborative culture, academic achievement, and classroom management. Stobaugh (2023) writes:

> In addition to increasing academic performance, physical activity interventions enhance executive-function skills including working memory, flexible

> thinking, and self-control in children (Egger, Conzelmann, & Schmidt, 2018; Schmidt, Jäger, Egger, Roebers, & Conzelmann, 2015). These core executive functions are foundational for students' social, physical, psychological, and emotional development. Researchers Mirko Schmidt and colleagues (2017) assert that appropriate development in these areas is positively associated with school readiness and academic achievement. . . . Movement has a positive impact on academic achievement for students of all ages. (p. 16)

We know students benefit from movement, and that benefit is seen in their learning. When students have a chance to partake in some physical activity, they are ready to try the hard stuff, to show up for cognitively demanding tasks. Movement sets students up to be engaged in the learning process.

Consider the following ideas for embedding movement into lessons built around essential skills.

- When facilitating a whole-class discussion, post prompts relevant to the lesson around the room, read them aloud, and then instruct students to stand by the prompt they wish to contribute to. Give students time to confer with one another, and then facilitate a discussion, offering each group a turn to chime in.
- After students work independently to complete a chart, organizer, or worksheet, allow them to work with a partner to compare their findings. Based on your space and time constraints, students may stand, walk around the room, or engage in other types of movement on the school grounds (in a hallway, gym, courtyard, field, or other open space).
- Pick your favorite classroom game that includes movement, and structure it around a review of the essential skills students have practiced in the most recent lesson.

Incorporating movement into instruction is simple and makes a noticeable difference in student engagement; plus, teachers can get students moving without investing in extra resources or taking time away from the lessons. While some movement strategies require more thought and planning, the most basic way to get started is to routinely allow students to pair off and stand up or walk around as they share their findings, discuss possibilities, and collaborate to complete a task. Part 2 (page 49) of this book includes ideas for allowing students to work in pairs or groups. Experiment with incorporating movement during this portion of the lesson.

CHAPTER 3

UNPACK ACADEMIC STANDARDS TO IDENTIFY ESSENTIAL SKILLS

High-quality and consistent standards for all students are necessary to ensure that all students learn at high levels. Academic standards provide a road map to learning. Teachers look to the standards to identify the essential skills students need and to inform their instruction. We know it is essential to determine a specific set of uniform standards to keep the learning consistent.

Teachers in the United States saw this drive to unify standards with the introduction of the Common Core. The Common Core State Standards, introduced in 2009, aimed to ensure that each student graduates "from high school with the skills and knowledge necessary to succeed in college, career, and life, regardless of where they live" (Common Core State Standards Initiative, n.d.). While most states initially adopted the standards, over time, they found various reasons to revise them, edit them, or create their own sets of academic standards (McKneely, 2020).

For example, the Wisconsin Department of Public Instruction (n.d.a) has created the Wisconsin Academic Standards, the California State Board of Education (2022) uses the California Content Standards, the Wyoming Department of Education (n.d.) utilizes the Wyoming Content and Performance Standards, and the Massachusetts Department of Elementary and Secondary Education (2022) has frameworks for each of its content areas, to name a few.

Whatever moniker your state or province uses for academic standards, consider them a vital part of your district's mission and vision statements. Many school districts highlight their benchmarks and rigorous standards in their mission and vision statements, explaining the goal of preparing all students for success in college and career. The important work for teachers and their teams is to unpack their state's or province's standards and backward plan to equip students with the skills they'll need to achieve at high levels on benchmarks during their time in K–12, in higher education, and along their chosen career path.

In this chapter, I explain the process my team and I developed to unpack academic standards and compile the list of seven essential skills I use in this book. I provide a template for you to design your own process. I also explain why establishing vigorous learning intentions and writing scaffolded success criteria are essential for embedding essential skills into instruction. Finally, I provide guidance you can use to start writing your own learning intentions and success criteria as you begin working with essential skills.

Unpacking Academic Standards

In the introduction (page 1), I outlined the seven literacy skills I use in this book. In this section, I share how I identified those seven skills as the focus of essential literacy instruction for K–12 students in my school.

In my early years of instructional coaching, my school in Wisconsin did not intentionally teach toward a specific set of essential skills. Like all states, we had our own educational standards. In professional development, we would review the state standards and discuss their implementation. However, most teachers relied heavily on their course guides, unit plans, course-alike colleagues, and expertise to teach their content area.

Undertaking the process to unpack the state standards, identify essential skills, and embed them in classroom instruction was born out of necessity. As a school, we knew a high ACT score was necessary for our college-bound students, and important to our non-college-bound students as well. We knew we needed to raise our reading scores for the ACT, and were sufficiently behind the state average at the time.

I created a committee tasked with composing a list of essential skills that students needed to be successful. Eventually, these essential skills would become the cornerstone of teachers' learning intentions and scaffolded success criteria. This committee was made up of at least one teacher from each department. Also, I specifically encouraged novice teachers and veteran teachers to join us in this effort. I wanted the voices of our novice teachers and their ideas and suggestions since they were our most recent college graduates. I also needed the experience and expertise of our veteran teachers to support us in this new initiative.

First, we created a brief survey asking all classroom teachers what skills they deemed most necessary (most essential). We did not give them a list of skills. We wanted their responses to be organic; we wanted them to give us the skills they deemed most necessary in their content area. Here are a few of their most common responses. (I have rewritten responses for clarity.)

- Read critically for comprehension.
- Understand and use compare-and-contrast statements.
- Read a variety of sources for information and for pleasure.
- Make inferences and draw conclusions.
- Find the main idea and details of a text.
- Take effective notes in class.
- Make effective summary notes for studying.
- Define and give multiple examples of content-based vocabulary.
- Use academic vocabulary in writing.
- Be able to evaluate arguments.

Our committee chose the following key language we saw most often repeated by teachers.

1. Compare and contrast.
2. Infer.
3. Identify main idea and detail.
4. Summarize.
5. Use vocabulary.
6. Evaluate arguments.
7. Understand cause and effect.

Armed with these key words, we gathered two specific documents: (1) the ACT College and Career Readiness Standards for Reading (ACT, n.d.), score range 16–32, and (2) the Common Core State Standards for English Language Arts and Literacy in History/Social Studies, Science, and Technical Subjects (National Governors Association Center for Best Practices [NGA] & Council of Chief State School Officers [CCSSO], 2010).

Our team highlighted skills from the ACT standards that aligned with the list our teachers compiled. We highlighted the following essential skills.

- Locating and identifying the main idea
- Finding supporting details
- Drawing conclusions
- Understanding and analyzing words and their meanings
- Using and understanding inference
- Making comparisons between and among texts

Besides the ACT, we also looked for standards overlap in the Common Core State Standards, specifically the Common Core English language arts (ELA) standards for reading informational text, grades 9–12 (NGA & CCSSO, 2010). At that time, we did not utilize the Wisconsin Academic Standards because the state still used the Common Core. Within those standards, we saw similar headings: Key Ideas and Details, Craft and Structure, and Integration of Knowledge and Ideas. In addition, we saw comparable language from our teachers' list and from the ACT: determining a central idea, providing details, writing a summary, determining the meaning of words and phrases, determining an author's point of view and purpose, and evaluating arguments.

After we had chosen our standards, I wanted to see the standards from other states to determine whether the pattern was consistent across the country. Were our standards random, or was there similar language in other states' standards? I chose California, Indiana, and Maine so that I had a representative from the West, Midwest, and East regions of the nation. As I perused the College and Career Readiness Anchor Standards for Reading for the state of California, I read this anchor standard for ELA, grades 6–12: "Read closely to determine what the text says explicitly and to make logical inferences from it; cite specific textual evidence when writing or speaking to support conclusions drawn from the text" (Key Ideas and Details 1; California Department of Education, 2013, p. 46).

This skill also showed up when I reviewed the Indiana Department of Education's (2020) Indiana Academic Standards for English Language Arts, grades 9–10.

Under the heading Reading: Literature and subheading Key Ideas and Textual Support, I read, "Analyze what a text says both explicitly and implicitly as well as inferences and interpretations through citing strong and thorough textual evidence" (9–10.RL.2.1; Indiana Department of Education, 2020, p. 156).

Finally, I reviewed the Maine Department of Education's (2020) Maine Learning Results English Language Arts Standards. If you look under ELA in Common Format, you will find a chart of the standards. Within the strand Reading: Key Ideas and Details, the standard is this: "Read various texts closely to determine what each text explicitly says and to make logical inferences; cite specific textual evidence to support conclusions drawn from the texts" (R.4; Maine Department of Education, 2020).

Across the West, Midwest, and East, I saw a familiar set of essential skills all students need to be successful. While some academic standards may be unique to a specific district or region, essential skills are deeply rooted in the basics of strong thinking skills.

Utilizing the list created by our teachers; the ACT reading standards, score range 16–32; and the Common Core English language arts standards for reading informational text, grades 9–12, we created our list of the following seven essential skills.

1. Locate the main idea and identify supporting details.
2. Compose a summary.
3. Interpret and apply academic vocabulary.
4. Identify and apply inference.
5. Identify and understand cause–effect relationships.
6. Identify and understand relationships using compare and contrast.
7. Delineate and evaluate arguments.

These essential skills became the cornerstone of the vigorous learning intentions and scaffolded success criteria we as teachers wrote for our classroom instruction.

Pause for a moment and reflect on what you've read. What stands out to you about the process my team undertook and the findings we uncovered? Would your school benefit from undertaking a similar process?

If you answered yes, consider the following template as a starting point for designing a process customized to your school's needs in unpacking your state's or province's standards.

1. Gather colleagues to undertake this process as a team. I suggest inviting a team member from each content area. Also strive to gather a diverse group of members to provide various perspectives.
2. Gather your state's or province's standards and the standardized test that is most used in your state or province.
3. Work together to highlight the skills most often repeated throughout your state's or province's standards and the standardized test.
4. Create a list of the most repeated skills.
5. Allow time for each member of the group to write vigorous learning intentions and scaffolded success criteria customized to their content area. Share these with the group, practice implementing them, and report back to the group about your results.

Customize this template as needed to suit the needs of your group and the goals you set for your school. As you unpack your state's or province's standards, don't hesitate to review other states' or provinces' standards. You will notice the commonality of essential skills as a worthwhile and purposeful guide to good teaching and learning.

If you answered no—if you're not in a position to undertake this process—it's OK to use the seven essential skills identified in this book. Focus your attention on establishing vigorous learning intentions and scaffolded success criteria suited to your content area and student needs.

Establishing *Vigorous* Learning Intentions

I briefly touched on establishing learning intentions and success criteria in chapter 2 (page 21) in the context of fostering a sustainable classroom culture. But how do teachers go about writing their learning intentions and success criteria in a way that centers an essential skill in the instruction?

When I think of the kinds of standards teachers need to guide their teaching, I find the word *vigorous* especially fitting. This is essential for holding high expectations for all students. Vigorous learning intentions are engaging, empowering, and (whenever possible) entertaining. And they provide a robust container for embedding essential skills that present meaningful tasks for students to demonstrate their learning.

Inflexible standards are not ideal; teachers need standards that are energetic and effective. Students need standards that support them to access real, relevant, and relatable learning.

What does it mean for standards to be strong, healthy, and energetic? *Strong* standards stand the test of time; they aim for learning that is relevant and enduring. *Healthy* standards are aligned with a dynamic mentality; these standards challenge students and engage them in productive struggle. Finally, *energetic* standards highlight the value of the work; they are written in such a way that students can't wait to dive right into the task in front of them!

Teachers must be empowered to apply standards to their particular context and their students' unique needs. How can teachers keep the intent of the standards but customize them for their context? Teacher and professional developer Carla Moore (2017) argues, "Clearly, if we have expectations for student learning that is rigorous, independent, and applicable in the real world, teachers need to be able to plan instruction that will help their students meet those goals." When planning instruction, we as teachers must offer students opportunities to take ownership of their learning. Students need the chance to demonstrate what they know in a creative and exciting way, working to highlight what they know and are able to do with increasing independence—meaning they're not chronically relying on the teacher to initiate their learning. In addition, instruction should be applicable to students' lives. The academic standards set the expectations of what students need to know and be able to do in a real-world context.

When you write your vigorous learning intention and scaffolded success criteria, keep the skill of the standard, but consider your content the vehicle for teaching that skill. As an example, let's revisit the vigorous learning intention and scaffolded success criteria I used in chapter 2 (page 21).

Vigorous learning intention: I can define and apply five art terms to critique a peer's work through a written summary.

Scaffolded success criteria: I know I am successful because

- I can define five art terms, including the word *critique*.
- I can critique a peer's work using the appropriate art terminology.
- I can write a summary sharing my critique with a peer for future help.
- I can verbally share my critique with a peer to help improve their work.

The content is a peer's work—that is, the vehicle through which the essential skill of interpreting and applying academic vocabulary will be applied. Consider another example from eighth-grade U.S. history.

Vigorous learning intention: I can cite the causes and effects leading to the American Revolution and debate those causes and effects with my peers.
Scaffolded success criteria: I know I am successful because • I can create a list of the causes that led to the American Revolution. • I can create a list of the effects of those causes that led to the American Revolution. • I can debate those causes and effects with my peers.

In this example, the content is the American Revolution, and the students will apply the skill of identifying and understanding cause–effect relationships when they debate those causes and effects with their peers.

These examples focus on the essential skills of interpreting and applying academic vocabulary and identifying and understanding cause–effect relationships. In the language of Moore (2017), these skills are rigorous, independent, and applicable in the real world, which makes them essential. Think of all the situations your students encounter where they draw on the skills of interpreting and applying content-specific vocabulary and identifying and understanding cause–effect relationships.

Vigorous academic standards encourage students to think deeply about the content they are about to learn and practice transferring skills both inside and outside the classroom. Standards that don't challenge students set them up for failure. Teachers need vigorous learning intentions based on the academic standards and scaffolded success criteria to plan lessons that move students from where they are to where they need to be.

Writing Scaffolded Success Criteria

Once you've written your vigorous learning intention, use it to create your list of scaffolded success criteria. What is the end goal students should accomplish in the lesson? What are the steps they need to get there? The answers to these questions inform your criteria.

Remember that scaffolded success criteria support students to monitor their learning and self-assess their work. When students self-assess, they determine the criteria they have mastered and the criteria they need extra help with.

Consider the following tips for writing scaffolded success criteria.

- Look at the essential skill within your learning intention. How will your students meet that goal? What do you want them to know and do with the essential skill?
- Scaffold the success criteria using a series of learning progressions to help students reach a specific milestone.
- As you write your success criteria, apply robust verbs that show progression. When students are able to move from *list* or *define* to *apply* or *construct* to *justify* and *measure*, you know they are making progress.

Notice how the following vigorous learning intention and scaffolded success criteria apply the essential skill of summarization.

Vigorous learning intention: I can summarize an article by picking out the who, what, where, when, why, and how and explain it to a peer.

Scaffolded success criteria: I know I am successful because

- I can read the article.
- I can write a summary by applying the who, what, where, when, why, and how details of the article.
- I can share my summary with a peer.

Notice how the essential skill of summarization is applied in the success criteria and what opportunity this offers students to self-assess their progress. If the students are able to read the article, they move on to the next criterion. If they are able to identify the who, what, where, when, why, and how but struggle to write a summary, they can look for resources to help with that part of the task. Perhaps students can use a graphic organizer to structure their thinking, work with a partner, or consult their notes. If students need more help, they can go to the teacher for assistance. Instead of looking at the whole task and feeling overwhelmed or stuck, students now have a road map of where they're going and the landmarks they need to hit along the way.

Embedding essential skills in instruction can seem daunting. But the tools you've encountered in this chapter ensure you can successfully navigate the process. Whether you need to unpack your state's or province's standards with a team or work individually to embed the seven skills in this book using learning intentions and success criteria, use the tools you've encountered in this chapter to support your next steps. Trust yourself in the process, and remember that this work is an investment in students that will support them to become stronger readers, writers, and thinkers.

CHAPTER 4

HARNESS BRAIN-BASED TEACHING TECHNIQUES

With essential skills, students gain the very important competency of reading comprehension. It's tempting to assume that if students master basic literacy skills and are on the path to becoming strong readers, this comprehension should naturally follow. However, it's not that simple. A major component students need to comprehend texts is background knowledge. When students have prior knowledge about what they're reading, they have a much easier time with comprehension.

Not only does research confirm this common-sense notion, but it actually shows that background knowledge matters *more* than a student's reading ability. In 1988, Donna R. Recht and Lauren Leslie conducted what has become an iconic study, loosely referred to as the "baseball study":

> Sixty-four junior high school students were divided into four equal-sized groups on the basis of preassessed reading ability (high and low) and preassessed amount of existing prior knowledge about baseball (high and low). Each subject silently read an account of a half inning of a baseball game. After reading, each subject recalled the account nonverbally by moving figures and verbally by retelling the story. (Recht & Leslie, 1988, p. 16)

As Recht and Leslie (1988) conducted their experiment, it became clear that reading ability had little impact on how well students understood the story. The piece that made the most significant difference was the students' knowledge of baseball. In other words, those students who were considered "low" readers did as well as "high" readers if they had knowledge about baseball. It turned out that a student's prior knowledge of baseball was the important connection to understanding the story.

What are the implications for teachers as they support students to become strong readers? Tutoring service Yup (2021) suggests on its blog that when teachers align their "curriculum with students' prior knowledge, educators can introduce more complicated topics and subjects with greater success." There are myriad factors teachers can't control about their students' learning, but we can control the kinds of reading materials we offer students and the subject matter they encounter to practice their skills. Think about how much more engaged your students become when they are learning about a topic they care about, have an opinion about, or even possess expertise on. If you're not already doing it, consider students' background knowledge as a major asset in literacy instruction.

In this chapter, we discuss the power of harnessing brain-based teaching techniques. We begin with the value of activating prior knowledge before turning to the science of learning to adopt brain-friendly practices.

Activating Prior Knowledge

Recht and Leslie's (1988) experiment shows how prior knowledge supports comprehension, but what is the link between activating prior knowledge and building new knowledge? Teachers must help students construct connections between old knowledge and new knowledge in virtually everything they learn. Professor of cognition and education Laura Wenk (2017) writes about this connection:

> New learning is constructed on prior knowledge. The more we understand about what students already think, and the more we help them engage their prior understandings, the more likely they are to learn well—and the less likely they are to misinterpret the material in our courses.

We hope for these connections in our classrooms every day and are especially grateful when students say, "This reminds me of . . . ." We look for any way to connect to our students' prior knowledge. I remember teaching freshman English students about *allusion*—a literary device authors use to refer the reader to a person, place, thing, event, or literary work they're already familiar with. When I shared this word and definition with my ninth-grade students, it was clear many of them needed an example. I knew I needed to connect to my students' prior knowledge for this term to take hold, so I turned to fairy tales to activate their prior knowledge.

I read the picture book *The Jolly Postman: Or Other People's Letters* by Janet Ahlberg and Allan Ahlberg (1986). In the story, the Jolly Postman delivers mail to characters familiar to my students: the Three Bears, the Wicked Witch, Cinderella, the Big Bad Wolf, and so on. As I read the story, many students nodded in recognition or commented, "I remember that story!" or "We had that book when I was a kid," or most poignantly, "I remember my grandma reading that to me." On nearly every page, they encountered an allusion to another story they knew. It didn't matter that I was reading a picture book to my high school students—by the end of the book, they understood allusion. They successfully activated their prior knowledge and connected it to this new bit of information.

In the early years of teaching this skill, educators bear the responsibility of activating students' prior knowledge. As we strive to help students make connections between old knowledge and new knowledge, though, we look for opportunities to move them toward independence. Professor and researcher Timothy Shanahan (2020) explains that students must become adept at activating prior knowledge for themselves:

> If I'm always providing kids with the appropriate background knowledge to understand each text used for instruction, then how do students ever learn to take on a text on their own? And, what can they do to take on texts for which they don't already have a bunch of relevant knowledge? . . . That's where strategies come in.

If we as teachers always do the work of activating prior knowledge for students, how will they ever be able to do that work on their own? Students will inevitably encounter texts that have no obvious connections to their knowledge base. Shanahan's (2020) recommendation to bring in strategies aligns nicely with my work. As an instructional coach, I'm always looking for strategies to offer teachers!

Consider the following strategies for supporting students to become adept at activating prior knowledge for themselves.

- **What do you know?:** Facilitate a class discussion about the topic of an upcoming lesson. Invite students to share what they already know about this topic, or ask open-ended questions to get students sharing. Write their answers on the board so that you're compiling old knowledge as a class. Consider offering students a graphic organizer if you want them to take notes. To support students to move toward independence with this strategy, allow students to take turns leading the activity throughout the year, offer bonus points when students demonstrate this skill on assignments, or build the skill into existing classroom routines that involve new content.

- **Password:** Look through a piece of informational text you plan to use in an upcoming lesson. Write key words from the text on index cards, and pass out two cards to student pairs. Students play a game with the cards, giving each other clues to help them guess the word that's on their card. Once students guess each password, they share one fact they know about that word or concept with their partner. To move students toward independence with this activity, allow them to help create the index cards for an upcoming lesson by suggesting key words.
- **Picture books:** Gather a stack of picture books related to the topic of an upcoming lesson. Invite students to form pairs or small groups; each group chooses a picture book to work with. One student serves as the reader, and another serves as the writer. The reader reads the book to the group. Afterward, the group discusses the book, pointing out words, phrases, or ideas that represent prior knowledge. The writer records the group's insights in the "Capturing My Thinking" graphic organizer (page 47).

Activating prior knowledge not only supports students to become strong readers but also offers opportunities for connection. Most students enjoy sharing what they know, feel proud of their interests, and appreciate the chance to be an expert.

Utilizing the Science of Learning

To support students in mastering essential skills for the long term, we as teachers can look to the science of learning. As neuroscience gains more insight into how the brain stores and recalls information, teachers can design brain-friendly strategies to work with students' natural abilities rather than against them.

What does brain science teach us about what the body needs to stay engaged in the learning environment? There are three key recommendations teachers can easily incorporate into the classroom that will make a big impact for students: (1) chunk information into smaller pieces, (2) practice spaced repetition, and (3) offer diverse opportunities for retrieval. Let's look at each of these more closely.

Chunk Information Into Smaller Pieces

Overloading the brain with too much information results in suboptimal learning conditions. Students learn best when they encounter information in smaller pieces. "The hippocampus has a limitation on how much it can hold. It is overloaded quickly, based partly on learner background and subject complexity" (Jensen, 2010). Chunking information into smaller pieces gives students a chance to effectively access higher-order learning.

The example of this idea that stands out from my time as a teacher is when I taught freshman English students who read William Shakespeare's (1597/2004) *Romeo and Juliet.* Imagine if I had expected my students to just read the whole play start to finish! No, instead, we chunked the play, reading and talking about it in small pieces. We began with the prologue, taking it line by line and discussing it so students could understand the nuances of the language, how the story might have been received in its original context, and how we might view it as 21st century readers.

Pause for a moment and think about the next lesson you will be teaching your students. If you haven't already done so, consider how you'll chunk it into pieces so students' brains are at optimal capacity to engage with the content.

Practice Spaced Repetition

Neural connections become stronger when students are cued to revisit what they've learned at regular intervals. Research shows that when these intervals are intentional and consistent, students achieve sticky learning for the long term. Educator and author Eric Saunders (2023) explains, "It is optimal to revisit a learning target over short intervals *and* long intervals scheduled at one day, one week, one month, six months, and one year" (p. 25). Build this periodic revision into your unit plans throughout the year to optimize student learning.

This is key when supporting students to achieve mastery of essential skills. Just because students have successfully met a vigorous learning intention and checked off their success criteria, that doesn't mean they'll maintain automaticity over time. To keep those neural connections strong, students must be cued to retrieve information at regular intervals. When planning your units, budget time to revisit essential skills you've covered at one-day, one-week, one-month, six-month, and, if possible, one-year intervals.

Offer Diverse Opportunities for Retrieval

Retrieval strengthens the brain's neural pathways, making information easier to remember (Queensland Brain Institute, n.d.). Literally, every time students are asked to access that information, it strengthens the neural connection. Use bell ringers, activities, assessments, games, and other creative opportunities to cue students to recall those essential skills. The more they practice, the more successfully they move toward automaticity.

During my twenty-three years as an English educator, I tried to make English literature as fun and engaging as I possibly could. The worn-out pattern of reading a text and then writing the traditional five-paragraph essay was not something I subscribed to; instead, I wanted to create opportunities where students could demonstrate what they knew and were able to do in intriguing and inspiring ways. One of my most successful lessons involved teaching Homer's (1614/1999) *The Odyssey*. My students and I read the first several books of the epic poem together, but then I gave students the chance to choose one of the remaining books and teach it to the class. Book 9, "In the One-Eyed Giant's Cave," tells the story of the Cyclops. One student group decided to be a news team—complete with an anchor, a weatherperson, and a sports reporter—and use the Cyclops story as their breaking news! Another group chose book 11, "The Kingdom of the Dead," and dressed up as a goth rock band, telling the story in their lyrics. Retrieval needs to be creative, engaging, and empowering, or else students will become bored and drained from the drudgery. Give them a chance to show you what they know—they will be excited to do so!

As you make a concerted effort to utilize brain-based research and brain-based learning in your classroom, you may want to share your findings and pool resources with your colleagues. Consider creating a brain-based learning and teaching group of like-minded educators who want to delve into this work as well. The following are some resources I recommend for getting started.

- Kieran O'Mahony's (2021) *The Brain-Based Classroom* provides more information about making classrooms deep-learning spaces for students to thrive.
- Henning Beck's (2021) *Scatterbrain* discusses the brain's role in boredom, creativity, and memories.
- Eric Saunders's (2023) *Stick the Learning* offers techniques teachers can build into instruction to help students access learning for the long term.

When teachers integrate brain-based learning techniques, they help ensure that students stay engaged, achieve automaticity with essential skills, and move toward mastery of Tier 1 instruction.

Capturing My Thinking

Instructions: Read the assigned text. In the first row, record key words you recognize. In the second row, write about other places you've seen these ideas (for example, in books, movies, shows, news, media, or real-life experiences). In the third row, write something you notice in the text that you'd like to learn more about.

Key words I recognize are:
This reminds me of:
I would like to learn more about:

PART 2

YOUR ESSENTIAL SKILLS STARTER KIT

CHAPTER 5

LOCATE THE MAIN IDEA AND IDENTIFY SUPPORTING DETAILS

Locating the main idea and identifying supporting details is a skill all students rely on to succeed in every content area and beyond the walls of the classroom. Education writer Shane Mac Donnchaidh (n.d.a) explains, "From the small print of an insurance document to writing a book review, the ability to filter a text and identify its central idea is as much a crucial life skill as an essential literacy-based learning objective." Therefore, locating the main idea and identifying supporting details is an essential skill indicative of success in school and in one's professional career.

The *main idea* is the central concept a text aims to communicate, and *supporting details* are those elements of the text that support the main idea by telling the reader who, what, where, when, why, and how. In terms of literacy, finding the main idea and supporting details is the starting point for working with a text. I cannot think of an essential skill that is more often used in the classroom, in college, and in the workplace. Finding the main idea is paramount to understanding and working with any text.

When students can't locate the main idea or supporting details, they are unable to understand the point, the gist, or the theme of the text, along with the details that make that text interesting and informative. Imagine reading a paragraph and being completely lost, unable to determine what it's about. When students encounter a complex text and reread and reread and are still lost, we as teachers must step in with strategies that can help them grasp the main theme as well as the supporting details—the who, what, where, when, why, and how.

To teach students to find the main idea and identify supporting details, first practice the exercise together and model the process for them. Begin by pointing out the title and noticing clues it provides about the big picture of the text. Next, read the introductory paragraph and notice the main theme discussed there. After that, read one paragraph at a time, highlighting details that provide clues about who, what, where, when, why, and how. Along the way, circle phrases that tie back to the main theme. After you've modeled the process, introduce the activity for students to engage with the skill.

This chapter offers two activities you can introduce to students that empower them to learn how to identify the main idea and supporting details of a text. These activities are also appropriate for students who have already encountered this skill but need to practice it. Each activity includes two ideas for using the activity with students as well as a classroom example, a sample lesson plan, and reproducibles.

Activity: Details Detector

The Details Detector activity offers students a chance to find the main idea and subsequent details in a piece of text. The value of this essential skill cannot be minimized since "finding the main idea of a paragraph or longer passage of text is one of the most important reading skills to master, along with concepts like making an inference, finding the author's purpose, or understanding vocabulary words in context" (Roell, 2019a). This skill is necessary in all content areas where students are expected to interact with text.

The goal of the Details Detector is to help students keep track of their thinking in finding the main idea and the subsequent details. Start small so students can practice the skill; as students become more comfortable, add more detail boxes to the graphic organizer included in this activity, if you wish, or ask students to add more if they deem it necessary.

To complete this activity, show students an image or video of a treasure hunter using a metal detector to search for gold. Tell students that, like the treasure hunter uses a metal detector to identify the presence of metallic objects, they will search to locate the main idea and supporting details within a written text. The reproducible "Details Detector Graphic Organizer" (page 61) contains a tool teachers can offer students to record their main idea and supporting details.

Consider the following ideas for using this activity with students.

Idea: Chunk Texts

Chunk texts into smaller portions when first introducing this skill. This makes the exercise more accessible and allows students to practice with an entry-level task. In addition, students get the added bonus of working in pairs and collaborating with peers to comprehend text. The following instructions offer a basic template for this exercise, which you can customize for your particular context.

1. Break a complex text into paragraphs.
2. Divide students into pairs, assign each pair one paragraph to work with, and provide the "Details Detector Graphic Organizer" (page 61).
3. Ask each pair to read their paragraph and then work together to determine the main idea and four supporting details.
4. Instruct students to record their main idea and supporting details in their graphic organizer.
5. When all pairs have completed the work, invite them to share that work in a whole-class discussion. They have now accessed the text you gave them in an engaging and more comprehensive way.

Consider using the "Details Detector Graphic Organizer" as a formative tool. After giving students several opportunities to practice locating the main idea and subsequent details with peers, give students a new piece of text and assign them to complete the activity independently. Walk around the room and observe students as they complete this task on their own for the first time. Notice which students lack confidence or seem in need of extra support to complete the assignment.

This is a great time to have a one-on-one miniconference. Ask the student what is difficult for them. Is it the reading itself or finding the main idea and subsequent details? If the reading is too complex for the student, that may require an interventionist's help. However, if the student is capable of reading the text but is unable to find the main idea and subsequent details, they will benefit from additional practice working with the graphic organizer. In this case, I recommend creating a small group of students who are struggling with this skill. Provide this group specific and explicit practice using the chunking-text idea, offering them support to move toward mastery.

Idea: Handle Complex Texts

Use this idea after deliberate practice with chunking texts. This offers students the chance to handle a complex text on their own before collaborating with peers to create a visual representation of the main idea and supporting details.

Use the following instructions as a template, and adjust the exercise as needed to fit your lesson.

1. Provide students with a passage to read, and instruct them to identify the main idea and four supporting details.
2. Divide students into groups of three, providing each group with poster paper.
3. Instruct students to create a concept map on their poster paper to represent their main idea and supporting details.
4. Hang the poster paper around the room, and ask students to do a gallery walk of the main idea and details.

Consider using this idea as a formative assessment. Walk around the room and observe student groups as they complete the activity. If you see students struggling with this essential skill, create small groups to provide students additional practice and support with this skill. Designate a student who has mastered the skill to sit in with the group and offer their expertise to guide the group as needed.

Classroom Example

Ms. Aruna's students did not score as well as she had hoped on their most recent physical education assessment, which tasked them with writing a reflection about the main idea and supporting details in an article about jogging. As a result, Ms. Aruna plans a lesson around locating the main idea and identifying supporting details with her physical education class. She chooses an article about the controversial use of prosthetics in competition to explicitly demonstrate this skill.

Figure 5.1 shows how Ms. Aruna designs her lesson plan around this skill, including her learning intention and success criteria. To use this template to design your own lesson plan, access the "Planning Lessons Around Essential Skills" reproducible (page 62).

Ms. Aruna allows students to find a partner and provides each pair a copy of the assigned article and a graphic organizer. She instructs students to read the article with their partner, find the main idea and four supporting details, and record the findings in their graphic organizer. After students complete the work, Ms. Aruna facilitates a whole-class discussion in which pairs each share their findings with their peers. Figure 5.2 shows how one pair completes their graphic organizer.

Lesson Plan

Assigned text: "Racer Blades: Do High-Tech Artificial Limbs Give Athletes an Edge?" (Newsela, 2016)

Essential skill: Locate the main idea and identify supporting details.

Summary: Students work with a partner to read an informational article about high-tech prosthetics, locating the main idea in the text, identifying four supporting details, and justifying their responses to peers.

Grade level: Middle school

Vigorous learning intention: I can locate and identify the main idea and four supporting details based on the article and justify my response to my peers.

Scaffolded success criteria: I know I am successful because

- I can locate and identify the main idea.
- I can locate and identify four supporting details.
- I can justify the main idea and four supporting details to my peers.

FIGURE 5.1: Ms. Aruna's lesson plan for locating the main idea and identifying supporting details.

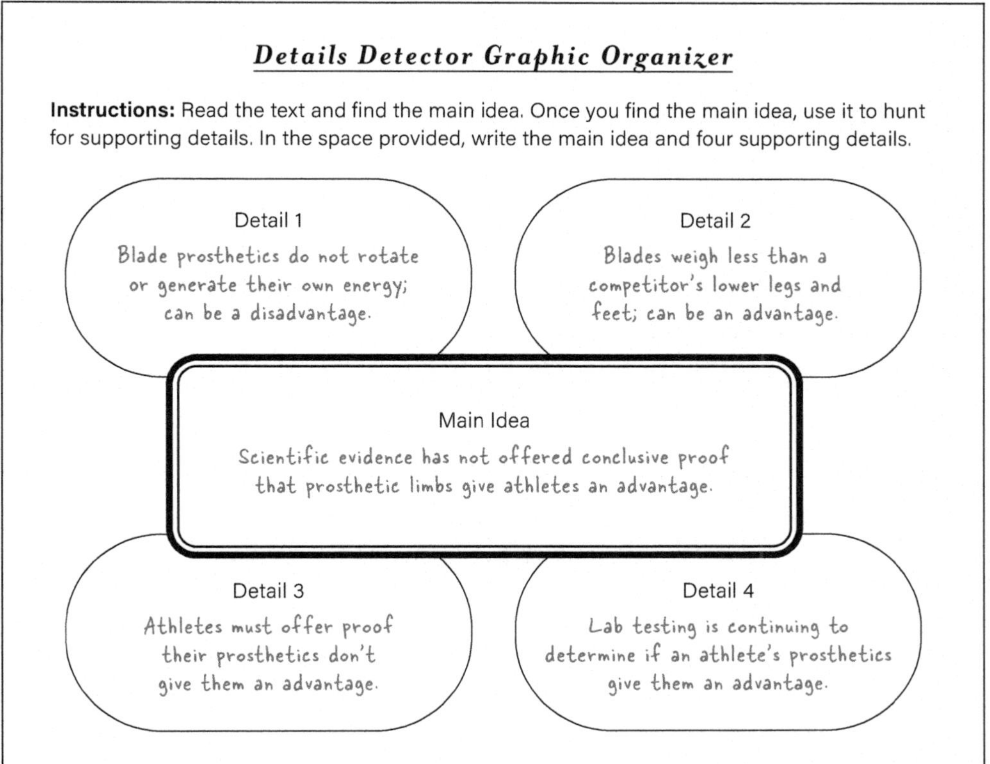

FIGURE 5.2: Sample Details Detector Graphic Organizer.

Activity: Main Idea With Supporting Details Organizer

While students use the Details Detector to track the main idea and supporting details, the Main Idea With Supporting Details Organizer activity goes beyond merely locating the main idea and identifying supporting details. This more challenging opportunity asks students to look for specific key words that help identify three types of supporting details: those that *explain*, *describe*, and *prove* the main idea.

Since "main ideas may be stated directly in the text or implied . . . you need to read a text carefully in order to determine the main idea" (Lumen Learning, n.d.); therefore, it helps if students are looking for specific supporting details, notably those that explain, describe, or prove the main idea. By applying the Main Idea With Supporting Details Organizer, students are compelled to carefully read the text in order to find those details.

The Main Idea With Supporting Details Organizer is more challenging than the Details Detector, so it's best used when revisiting this skill, rather than introducing it. I recommend utilizing this activity after students have thoroughly mastered locating and identifying the main idea and supporting details with the Details Detector. During this activity, students work in groups to identify the main idea and supporting details of a text. Each student is tasked with looking for a specific type of supporting detail: an explanation, a description, or a proof. The reproducible "Main Idea With Supporting Details Organizer" (page 63) contains a tool teachers can offer students to record their work.

Consider the following ideas for using this activity with students.

Idea: Find Explanation, Description, and Proof

Finding supporting details might be difficult for students if they're not sure what to look for. During this version of the activity, students look for three specific concepts that could help them find those supporting details.

Giving students specific types of details to look for provides helpful practice. When students know to go looking for text that explains, describes, and proves, they can more easily connect the dots to find the main idea. Therefore, this version of the activity tasks students with using a graphic organizer to find supporting details that explain, describe, and prove.

Adapt the following instructions as needed for your lesson.

1. Divide students into groups of three, providing each group with a text and the "Main Idea With Supporting Details Organizer" (page 63).
2. Instruct students to read their text and identify the main idea and supporting details.
3. Explain that each group member chooses which supporting detail they will find. (For example, student 1 will find an example of an explanation, student 2 will find an example of a description, and student 3 will find an example of a proof.) Students each look for an example of their supporting detail in the text, using the key words from the graphic organizer as cues.
4. Task each group with completing the chart, and invite them to share it with the class.

Idea: Identify Key Words

The key words students used in Find Explanation, Description, and Proof won't appear in every text they read, so they'll need practice identifying other key words that signal explanation, description, and proof. What other key words can they identify that introduce those ideas? Do they notice other words that help locate a supporting detail, such as *depict*, *clarify*, or *illustrate*?

In this version of the activity, students search for new key words that cue them to recognize supporting details, and they record those key words in their graphic organizer.

Use the following instructions as a template for the activity.

1. Divide students into groups of three, providing each group with a text and the "Main Idea With Supporting Details Organizer."
2. Explain that the key words that signal explanation, description, and proof are not always the same in every text and that students will practice identifying new key words.
3. Instruct students to read their text, identify the main idea, and record it in their organizer.
4. Have students identify their supporting detail and note any new key words that signal that detail.
5. Task each group with completing the chart, and invite them to share it with the class.

Locating and identifying the main idea along with supporting details is a critical element to understanding text. Students should be able to move beyond identifying the main idea and supporting details and practice working with them. As you read through these activities and ideas for implementing them, think about how you can use these graphic organizers in your classroom. In what ways might you modify them for your content area or students' unique needs? Also, consider how you might use these graphic organizers as formative assessments to gauge where your students are on the path to mastering the essential skill and what kind of support they need along the way.

Classroom Example

Mr. Rossi plans a lesson around locating the main idea and identifying supporting details for his science class. He assumes this lesson will be a review since his students are ninth graders and should have had plenty of practice locating and identifying the main idea and supporting details. He gives all students an article and a graphic organizer. He asks students to read the article, find the main idea and supporting details, and fill in the graphic organizer by providing examples of the three different types of supporting details: those that explain, describe, and prove the main idea. As Mr. Rossi walks around the room, he notices that all students can locate and identify the main idea, but a few students are having trouble finding the supporting details. Reminding himself not to make assumptions about his students, he begins to think about ways he can allocate more time to the lesson to explicitly model the types of supporting details and which key words to look for.

Figure 5.3 shows how Mr. Rossi designs his lesson plan around this skill, including his learning intention and success criteria. To use this template to design your own lesson plan, access the "Planning Lessons Around Essential Skills" reproducible (page 62).

Mr. Rossi divides students into groups of three, providing each group with a text and a graphic organizer. He explains that each person in the group will choose which supporting detail they will find: an explanation, a description, or a proof. Mr. Rossi tasks each group with reading their assigned text and identifying the main idea and supporting details. Students work together in their groups to complete the activity and fill in their chart. At the end of the lesson, Mr. Rossi facilitates a whole-class discussion, inviting each group to share their work.

Figure 5.4 shows how one group completes the graphic organizer.

Lesson Plan

Assigned text: "How Much Can Watching Hockey Stress Your Heart?" (Elsevier, 2017)

Essential skill: Locate the main idea and identify supporting details.

Summary: Student groups read an informational article about elevated heart rates during hockey events, locate the main idea in their text with three supporting details, and offer their own examples of key words.

Grade level: High school

Vigorous learning intention: I can locate and identify the main idea and three supporting details, selecting the key words provided and locating key words of my own.

Scaffolded success criteria: I know I am successful because

- I can locate and identify the main idea.
- I can locate and identify three supporting details using the key words provided.
- I can describe my chart and my key words to my peers.

FIGURE 5.3: Mr. Rossi's lesson plan for locating the main idea and identifying supporting details.

Main Idea With Supporting Details Organizer

Instructions: Read the text and find the main idea. Then find three supporting details: (1) an explanation, (2) a description, and (3) a proof. In the space provided, write the main idea (one to two sentences) and three supporting details.

Main Idea (What the author is writing about)	
The heart rate of hockey fans during a hockey game increased by 75 percent when watching on TV and by 110 percent when watching in person.	
Supporting Details (Information that explains, describes, or proves the main idea)	
Give an example of an **explanation** in your text. (Look for key words such as *after all*, *for example*, or *in other words*.)	"Their research raises public awareness about the potential role of emotional sports-related stressors in triggering cardiac events, and opens up avenues for future research into mitigating such risks" (Elsevier, 2017).

FIGURE 5.4: Sample Main Idea With Supporting Details Organizer. continued →

Give an example of a **description** in your text. (Look for key words such as *identify*, *portray*, or *depict*.)	"Previous studies have shown that cardiovascular events triggered by watching sporting events are more common in people with existing coronary artery disease" (Elsevier, 2017).
Give an example of a **proof** in your text. (Look for key words such as *because*, *as a result*, or *due to*.)	"Armed with Holter monitors, a team of researchers set out to assess the effects of a Montreal Canadiens game on healthy spectators" (Elsevier, 2017).
List additional key words that helped you identify explanation, description, and proof.	raises awareness about have shown that set out to assess

Details Detector Graphic Organizer

Instructions: Read the text and find the main idea. Once you find the main idea, use it to hunt for supporting details. In the space provided, write the main idea and four supporting details.

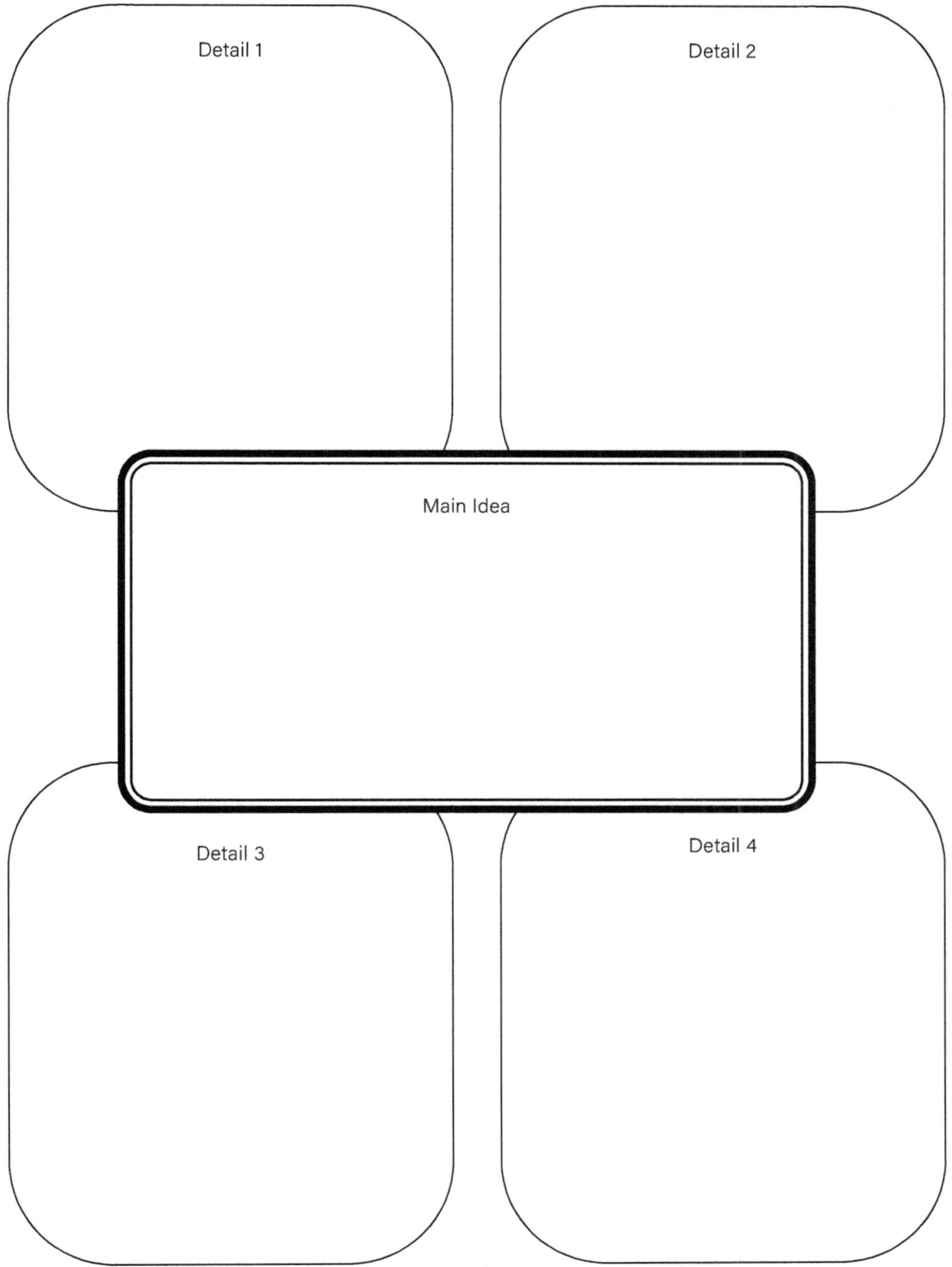

Planning Lessons Around Essential Skills

Use this template to plan your lesson. Be sure to note which essential skill you're building the lesson around, and include your vigorous learning intention and scaffolded success criteria.

Lesson Plan

Assigned text:

Essential skill:

Summary:

Grade level:

Vigorous learning intention:

Scaffolded success criteria: I know I am successful because

-
-
-

Main Idea With Supporting Details Organizer

Instructions: Read the text and find the main idea. Then find three supporting details: (1) an explanation, (2) a description, and (3) a proof. In the space provided, write the main idea (one to two sentences) and three supporting details.

Main Idea (What the author is writing about)	
Supporting Details (Information that explains, describes, or proves the main idea)	
Give an example of an **explanation** in your text. (Look for key words such as *after all*, *for example*, or *in other words*.)	
Give an example of a **description** in your text. (Look for key words such as *identify*, *portray*, or *depict*.)	
Give an example of a **proof** in your text. (Look for key words such as *because*, *as a result*, or *due to*.)	
List additional key words that helped you identify explanation, description, and proof.	

CHAPTER 6

COMPOSE A SUMMARY

Summarization is an essential skill that adults use every day in their personal and professional lives—often without even realizing it. Think about how often you read a newspaper article or a blog post and summarize it to your friends. Remember the last time you told someone about an awesome movie or show you watched, giving them the basic plot points while avoiding spoilers. You're able to do that successfully because you've mastered the skill of composing a summary.

The essential skill of summarization requires students to "determine essential ideas and consolidate important details that support those ideas" (Reading Rockets, n.d.b). Composing a summary demands that students identify which details are unnecessary and focus on key points; they learn to discern what information is relevant and how details are interrelated. Students must learn to recognize important information when they see it and then to organize and synthesize that information.

Summarization is a natural next step after identifying the main idea and supporting details of a text. Identifying the main idea and supporting details gives students a way to practice discerning essential information so that they can focus on organizing that information in the summarization skill. Summarizing is a complex skill, though, so students benefit from many opportunities to practice. As students become more comfortable with summarization, engaging with more complex texts allows them to demonstrate they can express what they have read in a discernible, succinct, and informative paragraph.

The art of summarizing can be particularly challenging for students. When they first encounter this skill (or when they don't have adequate practice with it), students tend to create a retelling, simply restating everything they have read. That retelling is usually a long slog of unneeded details that mask the necessary elements of the text. Students often fear they'll leave something out or confuse the reader, so they include those unneeded details. A summary provides the who, what, where, when, why, and how of the text, eliminating extraneous details. Students require explicit instruction, adequate practice, and enough experience to move to automaticity with this skill.

My go-to resource for teaching students to compose a summary is the 5Ws and H, created by literacy consultant Janet Allen (2008). The 5Ws and H give the students a structure to look for only what is needed without roping in unnecessary details that constitute a retelling. Allen's (2008) resource helps students accomplish this task by breaking down the process, giving each W (who, what, where, when, why) and H (how) a specific place, and tasking students to record details for each element. Once they've recorded those details, students use them to create the summary, drawing on connecting words such as *and*, *however*, *but*, *or*, *for*, *next*, and *then*. By guiding students to draw information exclusively from the 5Ws and H, teachers support students to move toward mastery of this skill. If students initially struggle to understand the difference, it may be helpful to display side-by-side examples of a summary written using the 5Ws and H and a retelling so students can see the difference.

This chapter offers two activities you can introduce to students to support them in learning to compose a summary. They're also appropriate for students who have already learned this skill but need to practice it. Each activity includes two ideas for using the activity with students as well as a classroom example, a sample lesson plan, and reproducibles.

Activity: Write a Summary From Details

In this activity, students use their "Details Detector Graphic Organizer" (page 61) to create a summary based on the main idea and supporting details they identified from the assigned text. I recommend using this activity after students have mastered the Details Detector. This allows them to experience the logical progression from identifying the main idea and supporting details to composing a summary.

Not only does this support students' conscious understanding of these skills, but it also affects the way students' brains map the process:

> [Summary] taps into key cognitive processes that encode learning more deeply: Students not only pay more attention to the information but also "mentally organize it into a coherent structure" and then integrate the information into existing knowledge networks, creating more durable memories. (Lawson & Mayer, 2021, as cited in Terada, 2022)

Therefore, taking the information from the Details Detector activity and using it to draft a summary of the assigned text gives students a chance to synthesize that information and communicate it in a concise and informative format.

Explain to students that composing a summary is a natural next step after locating the main idea and identifying supporting details. Explain what a summary is and is not. If introducing this skill for the first time, consider showing students side-by-side examples and pointing out the differences. The reproducible "Write a Summary Worksheet" (page 74) contains a tool teachers can provide students for crafting their summary.

Consider the following ideas for using this activity with students.

Idea: Stick to the Essential Details

Before prompting students to complete their assigned reading, reinforce the purpose of this activity: to focus on writing a summary without including unnecessary details. In this variation of the activity, students summarize an informational text. When introducing this skill for the first time, use a simple or straightforward text sample so that students can focus their attention on engaging in the skill rather than wading through complex text. Once students have adequate practice, they can work with more complicated texts.

Use the following instructions as a template, adjusting as needed for your class.

1. Assign students to read a text, and provide them with the "Write a Summary Worksheet."
2. Instruct them to construct a topic sentence based on the main idea and to list their four supporting details.
3. After providing adequate time for students to work independently, allow them to pair off and share their summary with a partner.

4. Leave time at the end of the lesson for students to reflect on their summary and revise it as needed based on what they learned from their partner.

Idea: Summarize Short Fiction

In this variation of the activity, students practice summarizing a fictional text. When introducing this skill, use a small text sample, such as a short story or flash fiction, to make the exercise more accessible. Once students have adequate practice and build their confidence, they may be ready to advance to working with a chapter from a novel or an act from a play. Summarizing fictional works can be especially challenging, as it's harder to eliminate unnecessary details. Offer extra support by giving students adequate time, space, and collaboration.

Use the following instructions as a template, adjusting as needed for your class.

1. Assign students to read a text, and provide them with the "Write a Summary Worksheet" (page 74).
2. Instruct them to construct a topic sentence based on the main idea and to list their four supporting details.
3. After providing adequate time for students to work independently, allow them to pair off and share their summary with a partner.
4. Leave time at the end of the lesson for students to reflect on their summary and revise it as needed based on what they learned from their partner.

Writing a summary can be challenging, and it's easy to veer into retelling rather than summarizing. However, by using the various resources in this chapter, students will be able to synthesize their thoughts into a coherent structure instead of applying unnecessary details that derail their thinking. Remember, the essential skill of summarizing gives students an opportunity to encode learning more deeply.

Classroom Example

Mr. Becker's freshman English class is studying Edgar Allan Poe's (1846/2021) "The Cask of Amontillado." After reading the short story, Mr. Becker tasks students with writing a summary. It's the first time students have summarized a text in this class, so he wants to assess their comfort with this skill. Mr. Becker sets a ten-minute timer, and students begin. As he walks around the room to observe students work, he notices they include unnecessary details. One student references the sound of Fortunato's cap and bells, and another notes that the servants all leave to make merry. More examples follow. After the ten-minute activity, it's clear that most students are struggling to write a summary, focusing on details that don't contribute to the main idea. Based on the class's discussion about the text, Mr. Becker knows the students are not struggling with comprehension; they simply need more practice with the summarization skill. As a result, Mr. Becker plans a follow-up lesson to explicitly teach the essential skill of summarizing. He will provide students with the "Details Detector Graphic Organizer" (page 61), altering it to include six details instead of four, so students can work with more information when completing their "Write a Summary Worksheet" (page 74).

Figure 6.1 shows how he designs his lesson plan around this essential skill, including the learning intention and success criteria. To use this template to design your own lesson plan, access the "Planning Lessons Around Essential Skills" reproducible (page 62).

Lesson Plan

Assigned text: "The Cask of Amontillado" (Poe, 1846/2021)

Essential skill: Compose a summary.

Summary: Students work independently to write a topic sentence and use their supporting details to craft a summary of the reading.

Grade level: High school

Vigorous learning intention: I can write a topic sentence and use supporting details to write a summary.

Scaffolded success criteria: I know I am successful because

- I can write a topic sentence based on the main idea.
- I can locate six details that support the main idea.
- I can use connecting words to craft my topic sentence and supporting details into a summary.
- Using the "Details Detector Graphic Organizer" and "Write a Summary Worksheet," I can compose a summary.

FIGURE 6.1: Mr. Becker's lesson plan for composing a summary.

As students complete the follow-up lesson, Mr. Becker is encouraged to see students improving their ability to compose a summary. He notices far fewer examples of students focusing on superfluous details. Once students complete the activity, Mr. Becker instructs them to pair off and share their summary with a partner. Figure 6.2 (page 70) shows how one student completes the worksheet.

Write a Summary Worksheet

Instructions: Use your "Details Detector Graphic Organizer" (page 61) to help you write a summary. Draw from your main idea to construct a topic sentence. Then write your supporting details in order. Use connecting words (*but, and, however, in addition, that, then,* and so on) to craft a summary that reflects the text you've read.

Topic sentence:
Montresor wants revenge on Fortunato because he says Fortunato talked badly about him.

Detail 1:
Montresor meets Fortunato at the Carnival and tells him he has a cask of Amontillado, but he really doesn't.

Detail 2:
Montresor asks Fortunato to go with him to his house to help him decide if it's Amontillado or not.

Detail 3:
Montresor compliments Fortunato to go with him and makes him believe he needs his help.

Detail 4:
Montresor takes Fortunato down to the catacombs to find the Amontillado. The catacombs are cold and damp.

Detail 5:
Montresor asks Fortunato to turn back since it is so cold and damp in the catacombs, but he only does this so Fortunato will want to stay with him and drink the Amontillado.

Detail 6:
When Fortunato looks into a dark hole where Montresor tells him the Amontillado is, Montresor pushes him in, chains him up, and starts to brick him in.

Summary:
Montresor wants revenge on Fortunato because he says Fortunato talked badly about him. One day, Montresor meets Fortunato at the Carnival and tells him he has a cask of Amontillado, but he really doesn't. Montresor asks Fortunato to go with him to his house to help him decide if it's Amontillado or not. He compliments Fortunato so he will go with him and makes him believe he needs his help. Then, Montresor takes Fortunato down to the cold and damp catacombs to find the Amontillado. Montresor asks Fortunato to turn back since it is so cold and damp in the catacombs, but he only does this so Fortunato will want to stay with him and drink the Amontillado.

When Fortunato looks into a dark hole where Montresor tells him the Amontillado is, Montresor pushes him in, chains him up, and starts to brick him in.

FIGURE 6.2: Sample Write a Summary Worksheet.

Activity: Write a Summary Using the 5Ws and H

This activity gives students the opportunity to focus on working with the supporting details of text and to get comfortable with noticing the who, what, where, when, why, and how. As they identify the details, they practice crafting them into a summary. Students can arrange the details in whatever way they feel is best, but they may not add new information. This is great practice for weeding out details that don't belong in a summary.

Students are often tempted to include new information, thinking that their paragraph is too short or that something essential is missing. They're used to giving long retellings and including extraneous details when they share their interests, so they need practice to master the skill of summarizing only the necessary details.

A key part of this activity is connecting the sentences in a way that is easily readable. Without fluent transitions, the paragraph will sound choppy and unsophisticated. To compose a well-written, fluent paragraph, students must practice finessing those transitions. Share examples, highlight connecting words, or point out nuances in syntax as needed to explicitly show students what a strong summary looks and sounds like.

Model for students how to look for supporting details to find the information needed to create a summary (who, what, where, when, why, and how) and how to put that information together for strong readability. The "5Ws and H Worksheet" (page 75) and "Somebody Wanted But So Then" (page 76) reproducibles respectively contain a worksheet and a graphic organizer teachers can provide students to work with their assigned texts.

Consider the following ideas for using this activity with students.

Idea: Find the 5Ws and H

This variation uses a graphic organizer to walk students through the process step by step. The students first find the 5Ws and H and then use that information to craft their summary. Encourage students to focus on using connecting words to create a polished and fluent paragraph.

Use the following instructions as a template, adjusting as needed for your class.

1. Assign students to read a text, and provide them with the "5Ws and H Worksheet."

2. Give students adequate time to read the text, take notes about the 5Ws and H, and compose a summary.
3. Allow students to pair off and share their summary with a partner.
4. Leave time at the end of the lesson for students to reflect on their summary and revise it as needed based on what they learned from their partner.

Idea: Use the "Somebody Wanted But So Then" Format

This variation is a great fit for fictional texts, as it's focused on a main character and supporting details about that person. To complete this activity, students work with a graphic organizer to collect the necessary details and then craft their summary. As with the previous variation, students get practice identifying only the essential details and communicating an entire story in only a few sentences.

Use the following instructions as a template, adjusting as needed for your class.

1. Assign students to read a short story, and provide them with a copy of the "Somebody Wanted But So Then" graphic organizer (page 76).
2. Give students adequate time to read the text, complete the graphic organizer, and compose a brief summary.
3. Allow students to pair off and share their summary with a partner.
4. Leave time at the end of the lesson for students to reflect on their summary and revise it as needed based on what they learned from their partner.

Classroom Example

Seeing that her students have mastered finding a main idea and supporting details, Ms. Aruna decides to use the same article (chapter 5, page 54) to introduce students to another essential skill: composing a summary. Figure 6.3 shows how she designs her lesson plan around this essential skill, including the learning intention and success criteria. To use this template to design your own lesson plan, access the "Planning Lessons Around Essential Skills" reproducible (page 62).

Ms. Aruna tells students they will be revisiting the article they read from Newsela. As they reread the article, they will investigate the details of who, what, where, when, why, and how. They will record their findings and write a summary of what they've discovered. She provides each student with a worksheet, instructing them to read the article again, take notes, and compose a summary. Figure 6.4 shows how one student completes the worksheet.

Lesson Plan

Assigned text: "Racer Blades: Do High-Tech Artificial Limbs Give Athletes an Edge?" (Newsela, 2016)

Essential skill: Compose a summary.

Summary: Students work independently to identify the 5Ws and H, using them to compose a summary of the article.

Grade level: Middle school

Vigorous learning intention: I can identify the who, what, where, when, why, and how and use these details to write a summary of what I've read.

Scaffolded success criteria: I know I am successful because

- I can identify the who, what, where, when, why, and how details in the text.
- I can record the 5Ws and H details in the worksheet.
- I can use the 5Ws and H details to compose a summary of the article.

FIGURE 6.3: Ms. Aruna's lesson plan for composing a summary.

5Ws and H Worksheet

Instructions: Read your assigned text. In the space provided, write information about the who, what, where, when, why, and how. Use the information you collect to craft a summary of the text. Use connecting words (*also, and, because, but, for, however,* and so on) as needed.

Who	Athletes with prosthetic limbs
What	Athletes with prosthetic limbs want to compete, but in 2008, the International Association of Athletics Federations conducted research to see if the competition is fair.
Where	The Olympics and other world races
When	2008–present
Why	Research hasn't decided whether it is fair to allow athletes using high-tech prosthetics to participate in competitions. The research is inconclusive.
How	This is a problem because athletes with prosthetic limbs might have an advantage because they are able to adjust their blades.

Summary: Athletes with prosthetic limbs want to compete in competitions worldwide. However, this might give athletes with prosthetic limbs an advantage because they can adjust their blades. In 2008, the International Association of Athletics Federations conducted research to see if the competition is fair. So far, the research is inconclusive.

FIGURE 6.4: Sample 5Ws and H Worksheet.

Write a Summary Worksheet

Instructions: Use your "Details Detector Graphic Organizer" (page 61) to help you write a summary. Draw from your main idea to construct a topic sentence. Then write your supporting details in order. Use connecting words (*but, and, however, in addition, that, then,* and so on) to craft a summary that reflects the text you've read.

Topic sentence:

Detail 1:
Detail 2:
Detail 3:
Detail 4:

Summary:

5Ws and H Worksheet

Instructions: Read your assigned text. In the space provided, write information about the who, what, where, when, why, and how. Use the information you collect to craft a summary of the text. Use connecting words (*also, and, because, but, for, however*, and so on) as needed.

Who	
What	
Where	
When	
Why	
How	

Summary:

Somebody Wanted But So Then

Instructions: Read your assigned text. In the space provided, answer the questions to identify the main character and supporting details. Use the information you collect to craft a summary of the text. Use connecting words (*also, and, because, but, for, however,* and so on) as needed.

Somebody (Who is the main character or protagonist?)	**Wanted** (What does the protagonist want?)	**But** (What problem or conflict does the protagonist face?)	**So** (How does the protagonist try to solve the problem?)	**Then** (What is the resolution or outcome?)

Summary:

CHAPTER 7

INTERPRET AND APPLY ACADEMIC VOCABULARY

To comprehend text at grade level, students must have adequate vocabulary aligned with that grade. In this book, I focus purposefully on *academic vocabulary*, those key terms that students frequently encounter in academic disciplines but don't use in everyday conversation. Academic vocabulary is critical to understanding text in all disciplines; without that understanding, students may become lost and frustrated in the classroom.

Interpreting and applying academic vocabulary is more than just memorizing what a word means. Students must go beyond rote memorization, aiming to interact with key terms and decipher their word origins and meanings. In studying academic vocabulary, students are exposed to "word origins, multiple meanings of words, and references to abstract concepts that relate and connect directly to targeted content areas" (Pennsylvania Training and Technical Assistance Network, 2019, p. 1). This robust understanding of vocabulary allows students to transfer those word origins and multiple meanings to other content areas and standardized testing situations.

In addition, fluency with academic vocabulary aids students in collaborating with teachers and peers in the classroom and serves them well in the workplace. If teachers want students to eagerly participate in learning, and to thrive as lifelong learners beyond K–12, they must equip them with this essential skill. Teaching academic vocabulary supports students to immerse themselves in the content and to collaborate with the learning community. Academic vocabulary is a mainstay in every classroom and professional discipline.

Without this skill, students struggle to comprehend and successfully interact with complex texts. Professor Lori Helman (2014) explains, "When students do not understand the terms for the concepts, they are unlikely to fully understand the material, nor will they be able to build upon foundational ideas and reach advanced levels of learning." When students lack academic vocabulary, many have difficulty interacting with the text and making meaning from what they have read. As a result, students read less because they find reading to be a burden.

This chapter offers two activities you can introduce to students to teach them how to interpret and apply academic vocabulary. They're also suitable for students who have encountered this skill but need additional practice with it. Each activity includes two ideas for using the activity with students as well as a classroom example, a sample lesson plan, and reproducibles.

Activity: Prefixes, Roots, and Suffixes

When students learn to recognize a word's prefix, root, and suffix, they go beyond rote memorization to understanding and applying the word in its context. The Pennsylvania Training and Technical Assistance Network (2019) explains how this skill offers students a tool to navigate encountering a new term in text:

> When students encounter unknown words, they can use knowledge of word parts (root words, suffixes and prefixes) to help determine the meaning. This is especially true when reading content textbooks because these texts often contain many words that are derived from the same word parts. (p. 2)

Imagine how mastery of this skill aids students in becoming strong readers, writers, and thinkers. Rather than ignoring a key term, shutting down, giving up, or feeling bad when they encounter an unfamiliar word, students know how to decipher it and engage with challenging texts. Literacy expert Sara Marye (n.d.) explains, "Students feel empowered when they understand the rules to the English language. Teaching Greek and Latin roots is just one way you can help your students understand the rules to our language." This ability to increase word recognition is not something that waits until middle school or high school; rather, Greek and Latin roots should be part of the scope and sequence in upper elementary grades. Knowing how to break a word into its prefix, root, and suffix is a valuable skill for students of all ages that will aid them in all disciplines.

There are many creative ways to support students in working with roots, prefixes, and suffixes, from note cards to board games. For this activity, begin by providing a brief overview of base words—stand-alone English words that use a prefix or suffix to form other words. As an example, *color* is a base word, but if you add the prefix *dis-*, which means "not," the word becomes *discolor* and changes the meaning. Teach students the difference between base words and root words: a base word doesn't need a prefix or suffix to be complete, whereas a root word has a specific meaning but cannot stand alone. For example, *aud* is a root word meaning "hear" or "listen," although it doesn't mean anything on its own in English. *Aud* forms the root of common English words like *audio* and *audition*—words that have something to do with hearing. This use of the activity focuses on root words, prefixes, and suffixes. However, you can easily expand the activity to include base words.

Provide a brief overview of roots, prefixes, and suffixes before you have students turn to practicing breaking words into parts. Once they begin the process, students often realize they already know some parts of words. It also cues them to practice reading skills as they encounter new words and decipher their meaning. The "Prefix, Root, and Suffix Chart" (page 87) and "Vocabulary in Context Worksheet" (page 88) reproducibles contain tools teachers can offer students for this activity.

Consider the following ideas for using this activity with students.

Idea: Consider Words and Their Parts

For this variation of the activity, think about the academic vocabulary words you want students to focus on in the upcoming lesson. Choose up to five words, and write them on a large piece of easel paper, indicating each word's prefix, root, and suffix. Reserve space to write what each word part means, labeling this space *Definition*. Provide students a copy of the "Prefix, Root, and Suffix Chart."

The following instructions offer a basic template for this exercise, which you can customize for your particular context.

1. Point out each word on the easel paper, discussing its prefix, root, suffix, and definition. Allow time for students to write the words and definitions on their copy of the chart.
2. Instruct students to work independently to identify two examples of words they know that have the same prefix. Students should repeat the

process for each root word, prefix, and suffix displayed on the easel paper.

3. When students have completed their chart, invite them to add their words to the easel paper under the root word, prefix, and suffix.
4. Continue adding to this chart throughout the unit.

Idea: Consider Vocabulary in Context

Choose a reading from your current unit, and identify academic vocabulary you want students to work with. In this variation, students look at how the writer uses the academic vocabulary in the context of the sentences and make educated guesses about what the words mean.

Consider the following instructions, and customize them as needed for your classroom.

1. Provide students with the reading for the lesson along with a copy of the "Vocabulary in Context Worksheet" (page 88).
2. Instruct students to read the assigned text and complete the worksheet.
3. Optional: Build in time between filling out columns 3 and 4 for students to pair up and discuss their work.
4. After students complete the first three columns, instruct them to look up the words in a dictionary, write down the definitions, and then construct definitions in their own words.

Setting aside time to explicitly teach academic vocabulary is a necessity for setting students up for success. Providing students this skill ensures they go beyond rote memorization to engagement with key terms and unfamiliar words. This essential skill is directly aligned to reading comprehension and achievement. We know if our students are successful readers, they will want to read more, and they will be more apt to read complex text.

Classroom Example

For years, Mrs. Pollard has taught vocabulary the same way—using a workbook to teach key terms. In each chapter, students receive ten words and use them to fill in the blanks, write their own sentences, or answer questions. Mrs. Pollard has also taught vocabulary when students encounter unknown words in an assigned reading selection. However, that usually consists of students asking her what a word means and her giving them the answer. She knows these methods aren't ideal, but she's not sure how to change this approach. This year, however, there are several new members in her department who want to try teaching vocabulary skills differently.

This group of teachers agrees to set aside time every day to explicitly teach Greek and Latin roots, prefixes, and suffixes. They will refer to the terms as "academic vocabulary," explaining to students why studying academic vocabulary is vital to their success as learners and future professionals in their chosen field. The group plans for the first academic vocabulary lesson by looking at their upcoming content-specific lessons. They read and highlight the academic vocabulary for their lessons and create a chart that focuses on roots, prefixes, and suffixes.

As Mrs. Pollard becomes more comfortable with teaching vocabulary this way, she notices all the roots, prefixes, and suffixes throughout the day—in a store, in a restaurant, and even at the auto shop while she's waiting. She brings that excitement to her students and encourages them to make note of the roots, prefixes, and suffixes they notice in their daily lives. To keep track of the academic vocabulary that students are noticing, Mrs. Pollard and her students create a word wall that showcases daily academic vocabulary terms and their meanings.

When it's time to study the U.S. Bill of Rights, Mrs. Pollard decides to highlight the academic vocabulary skill to support students in engaging with this complex text. Figure 7.1 shows how she designs her lesson plan around this essential skill, including the learning intention and success criteria. To use this template to design your own lesson plan, access the "Planning Lessons Around Essential Skills" reproducible (page 62).

Lesson Plan

Assigned text: The U.S. Bill of Rights

Essential skill: Interpret and apply academic vocabulary.

Summary: Students explore four words from the Bill of Rights, recognizing their prefix, root, and suffix. Students work independently to identify words that share these same prefixes, roots, and suffixes.

Grade level: High school

Vigorous learning intention: I can identify the prefix, root word, and suffix of vocabulary words used in the Bill of Rights and locate words with the same prefix, root, or suffix.

Scaffolded success criteria: I know I am successful because

- I can identify two words I already know that have the same prefix.
- I can identify two words I already know that have the same root word.
- I can identify two words I already know that have the same suffix.

FIGURE 7.1: Mrs. Pollard's lesson plan for interpreting and applying academic vocabulary.

Mrs. Pollard identifies key words from the Bill of Rights she wants students to recognize as academic vocabulary. She writes four words from the text on easel paper: (1) *amendment*, (2) *establishment*, (3) *grievance*, and (4) *infringed*. She breaks each word into its prefix, root, and suffix, indicating the meaning below each part of the word. As she begins the lesson, Mrs. Pollard provides each student with a matching copy of the chart. She reads each word aloud, breaking it into its prefix, root, and suffix and pointing out the meaning of each part. After introducing the chart to the class, Mrs. Pollard instructs students to identify two examples of words they know that have the same prefix and explains that they will do the same for each prefix, root, and suffix. She provides time at the end of class for students to add their words to the easel paper; this creates a resource that the class will add to throughout the unit.

Figure 7.2 shows how one of Mrs. Pollard's students completes the chart during the activity.

amendment		
Prefix: **Definition:**	**Root:** amend **Definition:** to correct; to free from fault	**Suffix:** -ment **Definition:** action, process
Example:	**Example:** amending	**Example:** payment
Example:	**Example:** amended	**Example:** encouragement
establishment		
Prefix: **Definition:**	**Root:** establish **Definition:** to make permanent	**Suffix:** -ment **Definition:** action, process
Example:	**Example:** established	**Example:** achievement
Example:	**Example:** establishing	**Example:** announcement
grievance		
Prefix: **Definition:**	**Root:** grief **Definition:** heavy, weighty	**Suffix:** -ance **Definition:** action, process
Example:	**Example:** grieved	**Example:** allowance
Example:	**Example:** grieving	**Example:** insurance

infringed		
Prefix: in– **Definition:** in, on, not	**Root:** fringe **Definition:** extremist views, marginal or secondary	**Suffix:** –ed **Definition:** in the past
Example: insanity	**Example:** infringement	**Example:** booed
Example: investment	**Example:** infringeable	**Example:** taxed

FIGURE 7.2: Sample Prefix, Root, and Suffix Chart.

Activity: Vocabulary Visual

Most students have a status quo relationship with studying vocabulary terms: defining a new word and using it in a sentence. Unfortunately, this approach does not provide students with the robust skill they need to engage with academic vocabulary across multiple disciplines. The Vocabulary Visual activity offers students an opportunity to learn, define, practice, and draw key terms.

Read Naturally (n.d.) explains that "students need a wide range of word-learning strategies that engage them in actively thinking about word meanings, the relationships between words, and how words are used in different situations." Creating those relationships with words helps students broaden their vocabulary. When students have developed those relationships, they are more apt to utilize their vocabulary in the classroom and beyond.

Teachers intuitively know how valuable visual representation is in helping students recall information. Education researcher Youki Terada (2019) explains, "Unlike listening to a lecture or viewing an image—activities in which students passively absorb information—drawing is active. It forces students to grapple with what they're learning and reconstruct it in a way that makes sense to them." Tasking students with translating a new word into an image is a great way to enact this meaning making. They create unique and personalized relationships with terms in a way that makes the learning stick.

Consider the following ideas for using this activity with students.

Idea: Interact With Vocabulary in Unit Text

This is a great exercise for boosting students' familiarity with academic vocabulary, as they get to interact with unfamiliar terms in a variety of ways. Students need various exposures to a new word before they can fully understand and apply it. When students work with words in diverse ways, they strengthen the brain's neural network. Over time, this increases recall and leads students to automaticity and mastery of the content.

For this variation of the activity, choose four vocabulary words you want students to engage within the upcoming unit. The reproducible "Vocabulary Visual" (page 89) provides a graphic organizer students can use for this activity.

Adapt the following instructions as needed for your lesson.

1. Assign students a text to work with that is relevant to your lesson, and provide them with a copy of the "Vocabulary Visual" graphic organizer.
2. Write four words on the board, and instruct students to copy them down in their graphic organizer.
3. Provide time for students to read their assigned text and complete their "Vocabulary Visual" graphic organizer.
4. Optional: Extend the exercise by giving each student a different set of words from the reading. Once they've completed their graphic organizer, allow students to form groups and share their work with peers.

Idea: Set It to Music

For this variation of the activity, task students with creating a musical rhythm (think of how you learned your ABCs). According to Florida National University (2019), "Studies have shown that music produces several positive effects on a human's body and brain. Music activates both the left and right brain at the same time, and the activation of both hemispheres can maximize learning and improve memory." As an example, when I taught *Romeo and Juliet* (Shakespeare, 1597/2004) in the early 1990s, I often played an abridged rap version of the drama. Students laughed out loud at the silly lyrics, but years later, I've had former students tell me they remember that rap!

Adapt the following instructions as needed for your lesson.

1. Assign students a text to work with that is relevant to your lesson, and instruct them to gather writing supplies.
2. Write five words on the board, and ask students to copy them down.
3. Instruct students to read their assigned text and compose a song including their five vocabulary words.
4. Optional: Allow students to complete this activity in groups, giving each group a different set of vocabulary words. Once they're finished composing their song, invite them to share it with the class.

Interpreting and applying academic vocabulary is an essential skill students rely on to thrive in K–12 and beyond. The activities in this chapter will support you to transcend the status quo teaching of vocabulary and offer students tools for engaging with academic vocabulary to become strong and capable readers.

Classroom Example

Ms. Campolo will be introducing binary compounds to her chemistry class in an upcoming lesson. However, she is concerned that students might be overwhelmed with the material; in addition to learning new vocabulary, students will encounter different types of compounds and must master new formulas. Chemistry has a reputation as a hard class, and her students find it a difficult science to master, so she wants to lower her students' anxiety as much as possible. She has surveyed her students to find out their comfort level with mathematics, specifically algebra and geometry. Unfortunately, the surveys came back with strong student concerns; as a result, it seems many of her students will be relearning mathematics at the same time that they are learning the chemistry concepts in her class. To support students through this process, she decides to construct a lesson around Greek numerals.

Knowing Greek numerals, specifically Greek numeral prefixes, is noteworthy since Greek prefixes can frequently be found in the English language, such as in the words *monotone*, *triathlon*, and *octagon*. Ms. Campolo wants her students to have fun with the lesson but also see its value in real-world situations.

Figure 7.3 (page 86) shows how she designs her lesson plan around this essential skill, including the learning intention and success criteria. To use this template to design your own lesson plan, access the "Planning Lessons Around Essential Skills" reproducible (page 62).

Lesson Plan

Assigned text: Binary Compounds

Essential skill: Interpret and apply academic vocabulary.

Summary: Students work in groups of three. Each group works to find the definition of one of ten Greek terms. Groups create a visual representation of their term.

Grade level: High school

Vigorous learning intention: I can define the ten Greek numeral prefixes and work with my group to create a picture of our assigned term.

Scaffolded success criteria: I know I am successful because

- I can draw a picture of one Greek numeral prefix.
- I can share my group's picture with other groups in a gallery walk.
- After discussions with my peers and the gallery walk, I can define and apply each Greek numeral prefix.

FIGURE 7.3: Ms. Campolo's lesson plan for interpreting and applying academic vocabulary.

Ms. Campolo introduces students to ten Greek numeral prefixes (mono, di, tri, tetra, penta, hexa, hepta, octa, ennea, and deca), which they will be using in chemistry equations. She puts students into groups of three, assigning each group to work with one of the ten Greek numeral prefixes. Students will define their term and work with their group to create a visual representation of it. After giving students adequate time to complete the exercise, Ms. Campolo facilitates a whole-class discussion in which each group shares what they discovered about the meaning of their term and displays the visual image they created. By the end of the lesson, all students have the chance to engage with the assigned vocabulary terms.

Figure 7.4 shows how one group completes the activity.

Vocabulary Visual

Instructions: Use the space provided in the first column to write your vocabulary words. In the remaining columns, define each word, write a sample featuring the word, record the sound of the word, and draw a picture that illustrates the word.

Word	Definition	Example	What the Word Sounds Like	Visual
Octa	The Greek prefix for 8	Octagon	Pokémon	STOP

FIGURE 7.4: Sample Vocabulary Visual.

Prefix, Root, and Suffix Chart

Instructions: Write each vocabulary word in the space indicated. Break the word into its prefix, root, and suffix, including a definition of each part. Then provide two examples of each part of the word.

______________________		
Prefix: Definition:	Root: Definition:	Suffix: Definition:
Example:	Example:	Example:
Example:	Example:	Example:
______________________		
Prefix: Definition:	Root: Definition:	Suffix: Definition:
Example:	Example:	Example:
Example:	Example:	Example:
______________________		
Prefix: Definition:	Root: Definition:	Suffix: Definition:
Example:	Example:	Example:
Example:	Example:	Example:

Vocabulary in Context Worksheet

Instructions: In the space provided, write the vocabulary word, the sentence it's used in, and how you would define it based on the context. After filling out the first three elements, look up the word in the dictionary and record its definition in the fourth column. Finally, write your own definition of the word, the way you might explain it to a friend, in the last column.

Word	Word in Context	Definition From Context	Denotation (Dictionary Definition)	Definition in My Own Words

Vocabulary Visual

Instructions: Use the space provided in the first column to write your vocabulary words. In the remaining columns, define each word, write a sample featuring the word, record the sound of the word, and draw a picture that illustrates the word.

Word	Definition	Example	What the Word Sounds Like	Visual

CHAPTER 8

IDENTIFY AND APPLY INFERENCE

Students need to master inference to thrive not only in K–12 but in the workplace as well. According to the Indeed Editorial Team (2022b), "This critical thinking skill uses prior knowledge and experience to connect unknown facts with known information. Examining inferences can help you comprehend situations and understand them in their entirety." By giving students adequate practice in the classroom, teachers support them to move toward automaticity, which they'll need to transfer the skill to diverse contexts beyond academic learning.

As an example, students are often encouraged to make educated guesses when they are responding to a question that has no apparent answer. Think about how often you use clues from your own experiences to draw logical conclusions throughout the course of the day. Students need explicit teaching and repeated practice to move toward mastery of this skill.

Shane Mac Donnchaidh (n.d.d) explains the benefits students receive when they can apply inference:

> [Inference] is a higher-order skill that is essential for students to develop to afford them access to the deepest levels of comprehension. Having a finely tuned ability to infer also has important applications in other subject areas too, particularly math and science. Given the centrality of pattern reading in these two subjects, it is no surprise that students will find these skills extremely useful in prediction and evaluation.

When we give students multiple opportunities to practice this essential skill, they will become adept at transferring it to other disciplines. Inference goes beyond simply guessing to thinking deeply and responding to questions with evidence-based answers, a process that requires comfort with prediction and evaluation.

Inference can be a fun skill to practice with students. As they make connections and look for inferences, you can see their critical-thinking skills emerge. It's almost as if you witness them ascending to higher-order cognitive processes. Robert J. Marzano (2010) says it this way: "In the last 20 years . . . we've become aware that some cognitive processes are foundational to higher-order thinking. Inference is one of those foundational processes." Although students need help to work with inference in an academic context, they generate inferences in their everyday lives anytime they ask questions, use evidence, or rely on reasoning to arrive at a conclusion. Students intuitively know how to look for ways to connect their prior knowledge to new evidence, so the teacher's role is to introduce and foster that skill in the classroom.

This chapter offers two activities you can introduce to students to teach them how to identify and apply inference. These activities are also appropriate for students who have already encountered this skill but need to practice it. Each activity includes two ideas for using the activity with students as well as a classroom example, a sample lesson plan, and reproducibles.

Activity: My Inference Example

The My Inference Example activity encourages students to use evidence and rely on their reasoning and prior knowledge to reach conclusions by reading between the lines. "Making an inference is a result of a process. It requires reading a text, noting specific details, and then putting those details together to achieve a new understanding" (Smekens Education Solutions, 2017b). When students can put those details together and make those educated guesses, they are more apt to transfer that ability to other content areas. Using inference to help break down text offers students a chance to connect what they already know and draw new conclusions.

When introducing this skill for the first time, define the term for students. For example, you might say, "*Inference* is a reasonable guess based on available information. Inferring is sometimes called 'reading between the lines' because the idea is not explicitly stated in the available information." Give students a chance to use their prior knowledge to set them up for success with new learning and share with you their thinking in making those new connections. The reproducible "My Inference Worksheet" (page 100) contains a tool teachers can provide students for working with inference.

Consider the following ideas for using this activity with students.

Idea: Go From Evidence to Inference

Identify a brief informational article or short story you will use as a primary text for your current lesson. Pull quotes from the reading, and use them to fill out the Evidence column of the "My Inference Worksheet." Provide a copy of the worksheet to students alongside the assigned text.

Use the following instructions as a template, adjusting as needed for your class.

1. Pass out a copy of the assigned reading to each student, and allow them time to become familiar with the text.
2. Provide definitions for unknown words students encounter in the reading, or use one of the activities from chapter 7 (page 77) to acquaint students with key terms that apply to this lesson.
3. Give each student a copy of the "My Inference Worksheet" where the Evidence column is filled out.
4. Instruct students to read each quote in the Evidence column of the worksheet and to write what they can infer about the quote in the Inference column.
5. Once students are finished, facilitate a whole-class discussion in which students share their quotes and corresponding inferences.
6. Optional: If introducing inference for the first time, consider also offering students thinking questions, such as, "What is the narrator's state of mind?" "Why do you think the narrator uses those words?" and "Have you ever been in a similar situation, and if so, how did you feel?"

Idea: Find Evidence for Inference

This variation of the activity builds on Go From Evidence to Inference and is best used as a practice activity rather than one that introduces students to the inference skill. Identify a brief informational article or short story you will use as a primary text for your current lesson.

Use the following instructions as a template, adjusting as needed for your class.

1. Read the assigned text as a class.
2. Provide definitions for unknown words students encounter in the reading, or use one of the activities from chapter 7 (page 77) to acquaint students with key terms that apply to this lesson.
3. Provide each student with one page from the assigned text as well as a blank copy of the "My Inference Worksheet" (page 100).
4. Instruct students to read their page of text, choose four quotes, and write the quotes in the space provided in the Evidence column.
5. Task students with working in pairs, explaining that they should exchange papers with their partner and complete the worksheet by providing their inference for each quote in the second column.
6. Once students are finished, allow them to share their work with their partner, or facilitate a whole-class discussion in which students share their quotes and corresponding inferences.

When teaching inference, I recommend applying the process: read a text, note specific details, and put those details together to achieve a new understanding. This skill can feel abstract to students working with it for the first time. Making the lesson fun and modeling productive struggle can help students be patient and feel confident despite the need for extra practice. Allow plenty of time for practice and call out small successes to keep students engaged.

Classroom Example

Mr. Becker decides students will continue to work with Poe's (1846/2021) "The Cask of Amontillado" (chapter 6, page 68) by practicing inferring based on select passages from the reading. Figure 8.1 shows how he designs his lesson plan around this essential skill, including the learning intention and success criteria. To use this template to design your own lesson plan, access the "Planning Lessons Around Essential Skills" reproducible (page 62).

Mr. Becker pulls quotes from the short story and fills out the Evidence column of the "My Inference Worksheet," providing each student with a copy. He facilitates a brief discussion about inference, providing the definition and an example, and he invites students to share how inference shows up for them at school or in their personal lives. Then he tasks students with reading each quote in their worksheet and writing what

Lesson Plan

Assigned text: "The Cask of Amontillado" (Poe, 1846/2021)

Essential skill: Identify and apply inference.

Summary: Students complete the "My Inference Worksheet" (page 100), reading quotes from the text and inferring Poe's intentions or meaning by making connections to what they already know about this short story.

Grade level: High school

Vigorous learning intention: I can define *inference*, infer meaning based on textual evidence, and justify my inference based on prior knowledge.

Scaffolded success criteria: I know I am successful because

- I can explain what *inference* means.
- I can point to textual evidence to support my inference.
- I can justify what I inferred by making connections to my prior knowledge of the text.

FIGURE 8.1: Mr. Becker's lesson plan for identifying and applying inference.

they can infer about the quote or Poe's intention in the second column. After providing adequate time for students to complete the worksheet, Mr. Becker facilitates a whole-class discussion, during which he allows students to share their quotes and explain what they inferred.

Figure 8.2 (page 96) shows how one student completes the "My Inference Worksheet."

Activity: What's the Subtext?

This activity works best with literary texts, rather than informational texts, and is a good fit for students who are already familiar with inference. What's the Subtext? is more challenging in that students are asked to analyze and take apart a piece of literature and put it back together again. Subtext is the underlying or implicit meaning of a literary text. Therefore, when students are identifying the subtext, they must analyze character, plot, and context. Writers "include subtext to add depth and complexity to a story in a way that mirrors real life" (MasterClass, 2021). Developing the inference skill includes the ability to notice and decipher subtext. Students need explicit instruction to recognize subtext, and they need repeated practice deciphering it.

My Inference Worksheet

Instructions: Read the quote in the first column. In the second column, write a sentence or two explaining what you can infer from the available information in the quote.

Evidence	Inference
"The thousand injuries of Fortunato I had borne as I best could . . ." (Poe, 1846/2021)	It seems like the narrator has suffered at the hands of Fortunato many times. He says he suffered a "thousand" times. That seems like a lot. I wonder what Fortunato did to the narrator to make him feel like that. I infer that he is so angry, he will do something to Fortunato to get back at him.
"You, who so well know the nature of my soul . . ." (Poe, 1846/2021)	The reader doesn't know the narrator; we just met him. But he says that we know him. I infer the narrator wants the reader on his side when he does something awful to Fortunato.
". . . punish but punish with impunit" (Poe, 1846/2021). (*Impunity* means to be free from consequence.)	The speaker wants to punish Fortunato and to make sure he doesn't get caught. I infer that there is something wrong with the narrator; that this thought of revenge has taken over his whole life. I don't think he is mentally healthy.

FIGURE 8.2: Sample My Inference Worksheet.

The reproducible "What's the Subtext? Worksheet" (page 101) contains a tool teachers can offer students for this activity.

Consider the following ideas for using this activity with students.

Idea: Decipher the Subtext

In this variation of the activity, introduce the concept of subtext, model how to work with it, and then offer students the opportunity to practice using a brief reading selection to identify and decipher subtext. When first introducing subtext, fill in the Evidence field for students with quotes that represent subtext. Students who are familiar with subtext and more practiced at recognizing it can fill in the subtext as part of the activity.

Use the following instructions as a template, adjusting as needed for your class.

1. Provide students with the assigned reading passage and a copy of the "What's the Subtext? Worksheet" (page 101).
2. Provide definitions for unknown words students encounter in the reading, or use one of the activities from chapter 7 (page 77) to acquaint students with key terms that apply to this lesson.
3. Instruct students to read the assigned literary selection and complete the worksheet.
4. After students complete the activity, allow them to pair off and share their work with a partner.

Idea: Create Your Own Subtext

In this variation of the activity, students move beyond deciphering subtext to creating their own by writing a flash fiction piece. Flash fiction is ideal for this exercise, as it's a complete story in under 1,500 words. In addition to crafting strong characters, plot, and setting, students must include subtext in their writing. If needed, provide students a few examples of strong pieces of flash fiction, highlighting how the authors use subtext.

Use the following instructions as a template, adjusting as needed for your class.

1. Divide students into groups, and provide each group with a writing prompt.
2. Provide adequate time for students to outline or plan their stories and write their first drafts.
3. Have groups share their stories with the class and invite their peers to identify and decipher subtext.

Identifying, deciphering, and creating subtext are the logical next steps after mastering inference. Subtext is a facet of human communication, spoken or written, and students need practice to recognize and replicate it. The activities in this chapter will help students become more expert at working with this skill.

Classroom Example

Mr. Nilsen decides to build a lesson for his high school music class around inference, using a short story as the primary text. He facilitates a discussion with the class to identify a learning intention and scaffolded success criteria for the activity. Figure 8.3 shows how Mr. Nilsen designs this lesson around the inferring skill. To use this template to design your own lesson plan, access the "Planning Lessons Around Essential Skills" reproducible (page 62).

Lesson Plan

Assigned text: "The Scarlatti Tilt" (Brautigan, 1971)

Essential skill: Identify and apply inference.

Summary: Students read Richard Brautigan's "The Scarlatti Tilt" and work individually to complete the "What's the Subtext? Worksheet" (page 101) before sharing their work with peers.

Grade level: High school

Vigorous learning intention: I can define *subtext,* give examples from the text in my own words, and provide proof to justify my interpretation of the subtext.

Scaffolded success criteria: I know I am successful because

- I can explain what *subtext* means.
- I can restate the text in my own words.
- I can support my interpretation of the subtext with proof.

FIGURE 8.3: Mr. Nilsen's lesson plan for identifying and applying inference.

Mr. Nilsen reads the short story and provides contextual information about the author. He hands out a copy of the reading and the "What's the Subtext? Worksheet" to each student. Students are tasked with independently reading the story again and then completing the worksheet, identifying two examples of subtext from the reading. Once students complete the activity, Mr. Nilsen invites them to pair off and discuss their work with a partner. Figure 8.4 illustrates how one student in the class completes the activity.

What's the Subtext? Worksheet

Instructions: Read the quote in the Evidence box. In the space provided, rewrite the quote in your own words or write a question this quote evokes for you. In the second row, write the subtext—the unsaid information you can deduce from the quote. Finally, in the bottom row, provide proof or state factual information that supports your reading of the subtext.

Rewrite the quote in your own words. (Or write what questions it sparks for you.)

This person is playing the violin. Is he any good at it?

Is his playing bothering someone? (The person says it was "hard to live.")

I wonder if this has something to do with the tilt of the violin. Is he not holding the bow right?

Is he trying to copy something from Domenico Scarlatti, the composer?

Evidence:

". . . with a man who's learning to play the violin" (Brautigan, 1971, p. 50).

What's the subtext?

A person is learning to play the violin. That could be noisy if he's no good at it. It could be hard to listen to, especially if he's not holding his bow right or trying to copy a classical composer. Practice with something easier.

Where's the proof? (Or what are the facts?)

A "man" lives in the apartment. He's "learning to play the violin."

Rewrite the quote in your own words. (Or write what questions it sparks for you.)

Why are the police there?

Did she kill him for learning to play the violin?

Why is the revolver empty?

She didn't run away. Did she want to get caught?

Evidence:

"That's what she told the police when she handed them the empty revolver" (Brautigan, 1971, p. 50).

What's the subtext?

It seems like the woman shot him for learning to play the violin. She couldn't take it anymore!

Where's the proof? (Or what are the facts?)

She handed the police the gun, and it was empty.

FIGURE 8.4: Sample What's the Subtext? Worksheet.

My Inference Worksheet

Instructions: Read the quote in the first column. In the second column, write a sentence or two explaining what you can infer from the available information in the quote.

Evidence	Inference

What's the Subtext? Worksheet

Instructions: Read the quote in the Evidence box. In the space provided, rewrite the quote in your own words or write a question this quote evokes for you. In the second row, write the subtext—the unsaid information you can deduce from the quote. Finally, in the bottom row, provide proof or state factual information that supports your reading of the subtext.

Rewrite the quote in your own words. (Or write what questions it sparks for you.)
Evidence:
What's the subtext?
Where's the proof? (Or what are the facts?)
Rewrite the quote in your own words. (Or write what questions it sparks for you.)
Evidence:
What's the subtext?
Where's the proof? (Or what are the facts?)

CHAPTER 9

IDENTIFY AND UNDERSTAND CAUSE–EFFECT RELATIONSHIPS

Cause and effect helps students go beyond the surface level of events to understand how they are related, to make meaning, and to answer the questions, "Why?" and "How?" It allows them to see human choice at work and to examine the consequences of human choice and the effects on people, society, structures, and history. Teachers in every content area use cause–effect statements every day to illustrate the relationships between events and processes. For example, a high school health teacher might ask students to analyze the effects of social media on adolescents. A fourth-grade teacher teaching a science unit might use cause and effect to help students understand how an object's speed affects its energy.

Shane Mac Donnchaidh (n.d.b) puts it this way: "Whether fiction or nonfiction, cause and effect are arranged in such a manner as to show the connections between a result and the events that preceded it. It can be thought of as the 'problem–solution' order." Students need mastery of this skill in order to make meaning of processes they encounter in K–12 and beyond. Understanding the connections between cause and effect is necessary in realizing and solving problems. Mark Galley (2020) from ThinkReliability explains, "Solutions solve problems, but the actual mechanism for reducing risk is *solutions control* causes. If you wanted to find all the different ways to solve a problem, you would need to know all the causes." Understanding cause and effect is essential for students to be effective problem solvers.

Students encounter cause and effect in elementary grades when they experience consequences of their actions. However, identifying and understanding cause and effect is also a skill that teachers need to impart through explicit instruction. Nancy Polette, professor of education at Lindenwood University, explains that it's important to understand "the relationship between cause and effect as a critical-thinking skill. 'Cause-and-effect writing works with other critical-thinking skills, such as sequencing, classifying, comparing, question-and-answer, problem solving, and decision making'" (as quoted by Brown, n.d.). Critical-thinking skills rely on understanding the cause–effect connection; as a result, students suffer when they cannot make the connection.

This chapter contains two activities you can introduce to students as they learn to identify and understand cause–effect relationships. These activities are also appropriate for students who have already encountered this skill but need to practice it. Each activity includes two ideas for using the activity with students as well as a classroom example, a sample lesson plan, and reproducibles.

Activity: Exploring Cause and Effect

In this activity, students read an informational text looking for causes and effects. Instead of merely underlining or highlighting the causes and effects found in the article, students break apart the text and make meaningful connections.

When students endure cause and effect in a real-world experience, it can often feel straightforward, but identifying the causes and effects in informational texts isn't always so simple. Sometimes when students find a cause in a piece of text, they assume the effect comes after, but that is not necessarily the case. In addition, authors can use a variety of techniques that imply cause or effect, so students must practice noticing these features when cause and effect are not explicitly stated.

Professionals in all disciplines rely daily on this essential skill. "One of the primary goals of education is to create empowered, analytic thinkers, capable of thinking through complex processes to make important decisions" (TeacherVision, 2019). When they master this skill, students are able to think through complex processes and make the important decisions. As teachers, we want students to be dynamic and determined citizens capable of making positively impactful and sustainable decisions. However, students cannot make empowered and informed choices if the relationship between cause and effect is murky.

When students do master understanding cause–effect relationships, they have the benefit of examining the forces that shape issues and topics they care about.

Think about tackling a school issue or a social justice issue and giving your students the chance to learn more about the causes and effects. This offers them a chance to become active participants in an aspect of their world, making their learning more real, relevant, and relatable. The reproducible "Exploring Cause and Effect Chart" (page 113) contains a tool teachers can provide students for engaging with this activity.

Consider the following ideas for using this activity with students.

Idea: Examine Cause and Effect in a Text

Choose a reading that highlights cause and effect for an upcoming lesson. Explain what cause and effect mean, and provide an example. When first introducing this skill, allow students to work in pairs for this activity.

Use the following instructions as a template, adjusting as needed for your class.

1. Assign students to work in pairs, and provide each pair a copy of the primary text and the "Exploring Cause and Effect Chart."
2. Instruct students to read the text and work together to identify five causes, recording them in their chart.
3. Provide time for students to complete their chart; leave a few minutes at the end of the lesson to facilitate a whole-class discussion in which students share what they've learned.

This basic version of the activity is an ideal starting point for students new to this skill. Ensure students master the basic concept at this level; from there they can practice it with increasingly complex text.

Idea: Examine Cause and Effect in Your World

In this scaffolded activity, give students a chance to research a topic they think is interesting. Perhaps students want to change the lunch menu at school. Give them a chance to learn about the regulations regarding school lunches (the causes) and how those regulations affect them (the effects). Also, give students a chance to offer solutions to their topic. In another example, give students a chance to brainstorm on social justice issues they find interesting to determine the causes and the effects. Of course, you will offer sage advice and wisdom and determine your school's stance and how to avoid controversial topics.

Use the following instructions as a template, adjusting as needed for your class.

1. Assign students to choose a topic of research, and task them with finding a primary text to work from.
2. Provide each student a copy of the "Exploring Cause and Effect Chart" (page 113).
3. Instruct students to read the text and identify five causes, recording them in their chart.
4. Provide time for students to complete their chart; leave time in your lesson for students to share their findings with the class.

If students have the opportunity to focus on cause–effect situations that are real, relevant, and relatable to their own lives, those relationships take on personal meaning. Students then have a chance to take action to shape issues they care about. When students can use this essential skill and make it meaningful to them, it takes on a more empowered direction; it helps students understand their actions and the consequences of their actions in a far more purposeful and fundamental way.

Classroom Example

Ms. Cloutier is the environmental club adviser. Students in her club have started several positive initiatives at school—from saving unwanted fruit at lunch and distributing it after school to collecting scrap paper at the copy machines to make scratch pads available for students during standardized testing.

Recently, her students have expressed their concern about the wildfires raging throughout the United States. While the school and the students are not located near the wildfires, her students want to tackle this subject because wildfires have an impact on the environment and the ecosystem.

Figure 9.1 shows how Ms. Cloutier designs her lesson plan around this essential skill, including the learning intention and success criteria. To use this template to design your own lesson plan, access the "Planning Lessons Around Essential Skills" reproducible (page 62).

Ms. Cloutier instructs students to pair up and provides each pair a copy of an article about wildfires in Yosemite as well as the "Exploring Cause and Effect Chart." She allows students time to read the article and complete the chart. After reading the article, completing the chart, and partaking in some purposeful discussion, her students decide to create an informative public service announcement to share with the school, explaining the causes and effects of wildfires and their impact. Figure 9.2 shows how one pair completes their chart.

Lesson Plan

Assigned text: "Yosemite's Giant Sequoias: Wildfire Threatens World's Largest Trees" (Cursino, 2022)

Essential skill: Identify and understand cause–effect relationships.

Summary: Students work with a partner to read the article and find causes of the wildfires in Yosemite National Park. They also identify the effects and write a personal reflection.

Grade level: Middle school

Vigorous learning intention: I can read the article, find causes of the wildfires in Yosemite National Park, and identify effects. I can make connections to prior knowledge in order to write a personal reflection and discuss it with my peers.

Scaffolded success criteria: I know I am successful because

- I can read the article.
- I can locate causes of the wildfires in Yosemite National Park and write about their effects.
- I can complete the personal reflection and share it with my peers.

FIGURE 9.1: Ms. Cloutier's lesson plan for identifying and understanding cause–effect relationships.

Exploring Cause and Effect Chart

Instructions: Using the assigned text, identify five examples of cause in the space provided. Then follow the prompts in the second column to write about the effects of each cause. Once you've completed the chart, take time to think about what you've discovered and write a personal reflection in the space provided.

Causes	Effects
"A growing wildfire in California is threatening the largest grove of giant sequoias in Yosemite National Park."	**As a result . . .** "at least 500 giant sequoias in the Mariposa Grove, including the famed Grizzly Giant which is thought to be around 3,000 years old," are in danger of burning.
"The Yosemite fire and aviation management department said it was 'proactively protecting' the grove by setting up a sprinkler system . . ."	**Which resulted in . . .** increasing "humidity around the trees" and "removing potential fuels from the site."
". . . thick smoke has worsened the region's air quality and obscured the park's scenic views . . ."	**Which led to . . .** "residents and campers near the fire" being "evacuated."
"Fire officials say that warm and dry weather conditions . . ."	**Therefore . . .** are "making it difficult to control the flames."
"Warmer temperatures and more extreme drought conditions caused by climate change are making wildfires more common."	**Consequently . . .** "officials say that more than 35,000 wildfires have burned across the US so far this year, which is well above average."

FIGURE 9.2: Sample Exploring Cause and Effect Chart.

continued →

Using your prior knowledge of this topic, the article you've read, and any other resources you've accessed, write a personal reflection about what you've learned. Why is what you've learned significant to you and the world around you?

Personal reflection:
Before reading this article, I didn't know anything about wildfires. I've seen them on TV, but never really thought about them before. I've never seen giant sequoias. I've only seen giant redwood trees on nature programs. It's sad that they've burned because it will take hundreds of years for them to grow again. This is another example of climate change and how it's impacting all of us. I wonder what will happen if there are more wildfires.

Source for article text: Cursino, 2022.

Activity: Proposing Solutions

Once students become adept at recognizing cause and effect in the texts they encounter, they can include the added step of imagining and proposing solutions. This is the natural next step when determining a consequence. Cause and effect most often takes on meaning in the context of a problem, so it's essential that students become practiced at seeing themselves as part of generating solutions.

In this activity, students go beyond cause and effect and propose possible solutions. Texts may not always provide obvious answers about how to solve problems, so students need practice, support, and resources (for example, authoritative sources for research) to complete this cognitively demanding task.

The Proposing Solutions activity gives students the opportunity to think deeply about a topic they care about and offer possible solutions based on the text and their background knowledge. In that way, the solutions become more possible and more feasible. We know that when a topic is engaging to students, they want to learn more about it. When we create interesting and thought-provoking lessons, students are more likely to engage in the work.

In the following two exercises, give students the chance to dig deep to learn more about a topic, or give them an opportunity to learn more about themselves and how causes, effects, and solutions affect them. The reproducible "Causes, Effects, and Solutions Chart" (page 114) contains a chart students can use for this activity.

Consider the following ideas for using this activity with students.

Idea: Find Solutions in a Text

This scaffolded idea challenges students to take the skill of understanding cause–effect relationships a step further by identifying potential solutions. By applying the entire process, students can see the beginning, the middle, and the potential end of those connections. Sometimes a reading selection will explore probable solutions, though that is not always the case. Encourage students to use educated guesses and problem-solving skills to identify possible solutions and conduct research about those solutions.

Use the following instructions as a template, adjusting as needed for your class.

1. Provide students a copy of the assigned reading and the "Causes, Effects, and Solutions Chart" (page 114).
2. Allow students time to work independently to read the text and complete the chart.
3. Leave time at the end of the lesson to facilitate a whole-class discussion in which students share their work and talk about potential solutions.
4. Optional: Instead of giving all students the same assigned text, provide students different texts on the same topic to expose students to diverse information, perspectives, and opinions on the topic of study.

Idea: Find Solutions in Your World

Curate a list of issues students will find interesting and relatable to their lives. These could be things happening in their school, community, culture, state or province, or local environment. Task students with choosing one issue to work with to determine its causes and effects and to identify potential solutions. Instruct students to work in groups to conduct research about their chosen issue and create a final product in response to their research. For example, they might design a flyer, an email campaign, or a letter to a representative to initiate change; they might record a video or podcast episode to inform others about the effects and proposed solution; or they might create a piece of art or write a song to bring awareness to the issue.

Use the following instructions as a template, adjusting as needed for your class.

1. Post the list of issues for students to consider and instruct them to choose one to work with, or allow students to find their own issue and submit it for approval.
2. Assign students to work in groups based on the issue they've chosen.

3. Provide students a copy of the "Causes, Effects, and Solutions Chart" (page 114), and task them with finding a primary text to conduct research about their topic.
4. Provide students examples of the final product you expect them to create, and encourage them to design their own.
5. Allow students time to conduct research, read their chosen text, and complete their chart.
6. Leave adequate time for each group to present their research and the final product they created in response.

Classroom Example

Mr. Gruene always starts class by asking students about their weekend or inviting them to share something fun they've done outside school during the week. Students often mention something noteworthy they've encountered on social media, although it frequently includes inaccurate or skewed information. Mr. Gruene wants to help his students become more aware of their source material and practice identifying reliable information. As a result, he decides to design a lesson about a social justice issue in which students will focus on cause–effect relationships. He chooses an article about the Salem witch trials to allow students to practice working with causes, effects, and solutions.

Figure 9.3 shows how Mr. Gruene designs his lesson plan around this essential skill, including the learning intention and success criteria. To use this template to design your own lesson plan, access the "Planning Lessons Around Essential Skills" reproducible (page 62).

Mr. Gruene provides students a copy of the article and a "Causes, Effects, and Solutions Chart." He instructs students to read the assigned article and record effects in their chart. Then students are free to work with a partner or small group to identify what caused the effects they noticed. Together, they discuss possible solutions, recording their work in their charts. Mr. Gruene calls for students to return to their seats and write a personal reflection in response to what they've learned. He ends the lesson by facilitating a class discussion in which students share their work. Figure 9.4 shows how one student completes the chart.

Lesson Plan

Assigned text: "The Last Salem Witch Has Been Exonerated, Thanks to an Eighth-Grade Teacher and Her Students" (Andrew, 2022)

Essential skill: Identify and understand cause-effect relationships.

Summary: Students read the article and use the "Causes, Effects, and Solutions Chart" (page 114) to identify effects. Students then work in pairs or groups to identify causes and discuss probable solutions.

Grade level: Middle school

Vigorous learning intention: I can read the article, find examples of effects from the Salem witch trials, and work with my peers to identify causes and brainstorm solutions.

Scaffolded success criteria: I know I am successful because

- I can read the article.
- I can locate effects of the Salem witch trials and record them in my chart.
- I can work with my peers to identify causes of those effects.
- I can propose possible solutions and discuss them with my classmates.
- I can write about my personal reflections as a result of my work with cause and effect.

FIGURE 9.3: Mr. Gruene's lesson plan for identifying and understanding cause-effect relationships.

Causes, Effects, and Solutions Chart

Instructions: Using the assigned text, identify four effects and write them in the second column. Work backward to identify what caused each of these events and record it in the first column. Then record possible solutions in the third column. Once you've completed the chart, take time to think about what you've discovered and write a personal reflection in the space provided.

Causes	Effects	Solutions
". . . her family was a major target of the Salem witch trials, driven by hysteria, Puritanical rule and feuding between families."	"She was one of 28 family members accused of witchcraft in 1692 . . ."	She was "finally exonerated last week after years of petitioning by Massachusetts teacher Carrie LaPierre and her eighth-grade civics students."

FIGURE 9.4: Sample Causes, Effects, and Solutions Chart.

continued →

Causes	Effects	Solutions
"Johnson said the devil appeared to her 'like two black Catts,' and she named several other people in Salem whom she said were involved in witchcraft. She also showed her knuckles, where it appeared fellow 'witches' had 'suckt her,' according to the 1692 examination document."	"Johnson was sentenced to death at age 22 . . ."	"Justice came in the form of a brief addition to the 2023 state budget."
"In 1711, after state officials realized they'd had little evidence to convict and execute or imprison women (and some men) for witchcraft . . ."	". . . they exonerated many of those who'd been convicted or even hanged . . ."	"LaPierre's eighth-graders set out on exonerating EJJ, petitioning the Massachusetts legislature with the hopes that a lawmaker would introduce a bill to clear her name."
"She petitioned Salem to be included in the act, which provided restitution to families of the accused."	"Johnson's name, though, was omitted from this list."	"Standing up for justice, advocating for those who cannot do so for themselves, recognizing that their voices have power in the community and the world, and understanding that persistence is necessary to achieve their goals."

Using your prior knowledge of this topic, the article you've read, and any other resources you've accessed, write a personal reflection about what you've learned. Why is what you've learned significant to you and the world around you?

Personal reflection:

While we don't have witch trials anymore, we have examples where people are unable to stand up for themselves and need help from others. Elizabeth Johnson Jr. was never a witch, but it was probably easier to confess, thinking they might spare her life. Today, we have examples where people aren't believed or trusted because of a lot of different reasons. We need to help those who aren't given fair treatment.

Source for article text: Andrew, 2022.

Exploring Cause and Effect Chart

Instructions: Using the assigned text, identify five examples of cause in the space provided. Then follow the prompts in the second column to write about the effects of each cause. Once you've completed the chart, take time to think about what you've discovered and write a personal reflection in the space provided.

Causes	Effects
	As a result . . .
	Which resulted in . . .
	Which led to . . .
	Therefore . . .
	Consequently . . .

Using your prior knowledge of this topic, the article you've read, and any other resources you've accessed, write a personal reflection about what you've learned. Why is what you've learned significant to you and the world around you?

Personal reflection:

Causes, Effects, and Solutions Chart

Instructions: Using the assigned text, identify four effects and write them in the second column. Work backward to identify what caused each of these events and record it in the first column. Then record possible solutions in the third column. Once you've completed the chart, take time to think about what you've discovered and write a personal reflection in the space provided.

Causes	Effects	Solutions

Using your prior knowledge of this topic, the article you've read, and any other resources you've accessed, write a personal reflection about what you've learned. Why is what you've learned significant to you and the world around you?

Personal reflection:

CHAPTER 10

IDENTIFY AND UNDERSTAND RELATIONSHIPS USING COMPARE AND CONTRAST

Students encounter compare and contrast early on in their education. Think of how many times you have taught students to compare and contrast without even thinking about it or explicitly priming your students to learn it. During a typical school day, you've likely asked students to tell you the similarities and differences between objects, pictures, theories, formulas, and so on.

Using compare and contrast lays the foundation for students to be strong readers, writers, listeners, speakers, and thinkers. It's a skill that helps them "improve vocabulary, describing skills, sentence structure, reading comprehension and more" (Project Play Therapy, 2021). In addition, compare and contrast prime students for high-level analysis of texts by giving them tools for greater discernment and understanding. Let's Talk Science (n.d.) notes that comparing and contrasting are important because they:

- lead to the ability to sort and classify
- help students to think about and focus on important details
- clarify the differences between related objects/events/concepts
- promote the development of organizational skills (by providing a structure for organizing thoughts and ideas)

- support habits of mind such as flexible thinking, metacognition, using prior knowledge in new/different contexts, clear and accurate communication (e.g., providing explanations)
- support the ability to evaluate (e.g., why one solution is better than another)

These benefits support students in all academic and professional disciplines. The reverse is also true—when students don't master this skill, they face a significant barrier to success in school and work. Students encounter complex ideas every day inside and outside the classroom; they need explicit instruction and practice to master this important skill.

One way teachers can support students in working with this skill is by cuing them to focus on how a text connects to them. Founder of Differentiated Teaching Rebecca Davies (n.d.) writes, "Helping students make text-to-self connections by comparing and contrasting is an important foundational skill. Teaching students to look beyond just surface level comparisons can help them dig deeper into their reading and build understanding." While the impact of teaching this skill at the elementary level is significant, the act of looking beyond the surface is something students at all grade levels need to practice repeatedly in order to recognize those subtle contrasts that may initially be difficult to find.

This chapter offers two activities you can use to teach students to identify and understand relationships using compare and contrast. These activities are also suitable for students who have already encountered this skill but need to practice it. Each activity includes two ideas for using the activity with students as well as a classroom example, a sample lesson plan, and reproducibles.

Activity: Compare and Contrast

This activity offers a great introduction to the compare-and-contrast skill. Because students take on specific roles and work together to complete this task, they can focus on the information and analysis rather than get overloaded. In addition, tasking students with a role offers them a chance to build their confidence. If a classmate is struggling, they can look for help from peers who excel at their role.

This specific strategy supports students to compare and contrast—to understand and identify relationships by recognizing similarities and differences. Shane Mac Donnchaidh (n.d.c) explains that "while the distinction between these two terms may appear on the surface to be quite subtle, it is important that students can accurately differentiate between the two concepts to ensure they are able to answer questions and prompts accurately."

In this activity, students practice identifying the relationship between two items using the compare-and-contrast skill. When students read about a topic that is real, relevant, and relatable to their lives, they build connections between their background knowledge and new concepts. Therefore, this activity's classroom example (page 118) gives students a topic they are familiar with—social media—and encourages them to make informed decisions based on what they read. The reproducible "Compare and Contrast Graphic Organizer" (page 125) contains a graphic organizer teachers can provide students for working with this activity.

Consider the following ideas for using this activity with students.

Idea: Work Together

For this exercise, choose two elements of your current lesson you want students to compare and contrast. Students will work in groups to compare and contrast these items, exploring their similarities and differences.

Use the following instructions as a template, adjusting as needed for your class.

1. Assign students to groups of four, and explain their roles: Student 1 will look for information about the first item. Student 2 will look for information about the second item. Student 3 will identify similarities between the two items. Student 4 will identify differences between the two items.
2. Provide each group a copy of their assigned reading and the "Compare and Contrast Graphic Organizer."
3. Give students ample time to read the article, complete their task, and share their findings with their group members.
4. Have students work together to complete their graphic organizer.
5. Facilitate a class discussion, or even a brief debate, by inviting groups to share and justify their findings.
6. Optional: Consider assigning each group different items to compare and contrast so that the class can cover more content and engage in a high-level discussion or debate in which they exchange more ideas and find opportunities to make connections.

Idea: Work Independently

For this variation, students identify their own items to compare and contrast. Their topic can be related to academic content or a personal interest. Provide students time to conduct research about their topic, and instruct them to complete the graphic organizer.

Use the following instructions as a template, adjusting as needed for your class.

1. Provide students with a copy of the "Compare and Contrast Graphic Organizer" (page 125).
2. Instruct students to identify two items from an academic or personal interest, and provide the necessary resources for them to complete research on their items.
3. Give students time to complete their research and fill in their organizer.
4. Leave time at the end of the lesson for students to stand up, pair off, and discuss their work with their partner.

These compare-and-contrast ideas offer students chances to work with similarities and differences in a scaffolded way—working both in a team and independently. In this way, students can lean on peers while they develop their confidence and ability with this skill, moving toward independence with time and practice.

Classroom Example

Ms. Garcia has witnessed several disagreements and fights break out in school because of students' interactions on social media. She and other teachers have shared their frustration with the principal. Instead of rejecting social media and trying to ban it, the principal encourages teachers to take a proactive and positive approach, perhaps occasionally embedding phones and social media in lessons. As a result, Ms. Garcia designs a lesson about TikTok and Instagram for her health class. This lesson centers on identifying and understanding relationships using the compare-and-contrast skill.

Ms. Garcia chooses an article about the similarities and differences between TikTok and Instagram to allow students to practice working with compare and contrast. She realizes this is only a first step in accepting the presence of social media in her students' lives, but she hopes that by creating more lessons focused on this topic, she will gain students' trust and respect. For this particular lesson, students will debate their preferences and aversions. Ms. Garcia hopes that by hearing from her students, she might be able to better plan future lessons.

Figure 10.1 shows how Ms. Garcia designs her lesson plan around this essential skill, including the learning intention and success criteria. To use this template to design your own lesson plan, access the "Planning Lessons Around Essential Skills" reproducible (page 62).

Lesson Plan

Assigned text: "Difference Between TikTok and Instagram" (Khillar, 2021)

Essential skill: Identify and understand relationships using compare and contrast.

Summary: Students read the article "Difference Between TikTok and Instagram" and determine the similarities and differences of these social media platforms.

Grade level: High school

Vigorous learning intention: I can read the article, find comparable and contrasting elements of the social media platforms, and share what I learn with my peers.

Scaffolded success criteria: I know I am successful because

- I can read the article.
- I can compare TikTok and Instagram.
- I can contrast TikTok and Instagram.
- I can determine which one I like better.
- I can share my results with my peers in a debate.

FIGURE 10.1: Ms. Garcia's lesson plan for identifying and understanding relationships using compare and contrast.

Ms. Garcia provides each student a copy of the article and a "Compare and Contrast Graphic Organizer" (page 125). She instructs students to read the assigned article and complete the graphic organizer. Next, Ms. Garcia invites students to stand up, pair off, share their work with their partner, and add additional notes to their organizer. She continues the lesson by facilitating a class discussion in which students share what they discovered, what their partner discovered that surprised them, and what questions they still have as a result of comparing and contrasting the social media platforms. Finally, Ms. Garcia sets aside several minutes at the end of class for students to engage in an entertaining debate sharing their preferences and dislikes about the social media platforms. Figure 10.2 (page 120) shows how one student completes the chart.

Compare and Contrast Graphic Organizer

Instructions: In the space provided, write the two items you're comparing and contrasting. In the first box, write two to three sentences describing how these two items are alike. In the second box, use the chart to list the ways these two items differ.

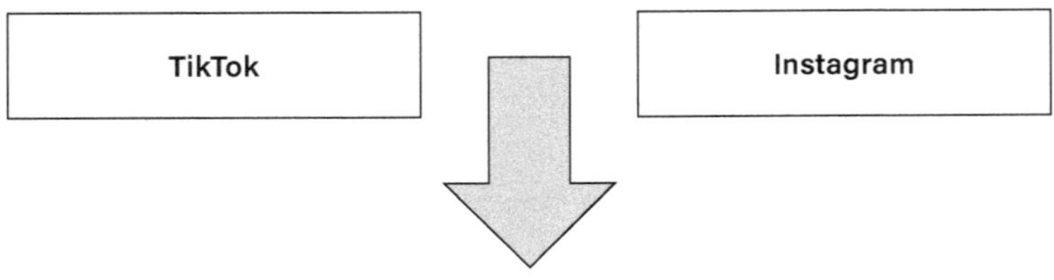

How are they alike?

Both TikTok and Instagram are very popular, and both started in the 2010s. TikTok and Instagram are social media platforms and both share short videos. Both use paid advertisers.

How are they different?

TikTok	Instagram
A stand-alone video-sharing app	Not a stand-alone video-sharing app
Owned by ByteDance	Owned by Facebook
Relies on its advanced AI capabilities	Focuses on the network layer and on explicit signals by users

FIGURE 10.2: Sample Compare and Contrast Graphic Organizer.

Activity: Compare and Contrast Informational Texts

Sarah Levine (2022), assistant professor of education at Stanford University, writes about compare and contrast in an article for *Cult of Pedagogy*:

> Cognitively speaking, contrasting similar things activates and helps add to your mind's map (also called a *schema*) of those things, which helps you

recall more details, make more connections, and develop more general rules about what something is or how it works.

When students have the opportunity to add to their mind map, they utilize all they have learned in the classroom and beyond and gain confidence in their ability to make meaningful connections. This activity allows students to practice comparing and contrasting informational texts—essential practice for students as they need to become adept at engaging with increasingly complex texts. This is particularly important for students as they engage with misinformation online. They must be able to discern fact from fiction, evidence from opinion, and pure intent from agenda. As an example, the revision and revitalization of family and consumer science education is noteworthy; what was once a class that girls took about cooking, sewing, and cleaning (the boys took classes involving drafting, woodworking, and metalworking) now focuses on "empowering individuals and families across the life span to manage the challenge of living and working in a diverse global society" (Wisconsin Department of Public Instruction, n.d.b). Part of that challenge is learning how some diets manipulate people and their health. Through this activity's classroom example (page 122), students will be able to compare and contrast the opinions of different subject-matter experts and the various diets discussed.

In addition, provide students with resources and tools to consider whether their sources are credible. I recommend the RADAR framework (https://libguides.sait.ca/RADAR; Reg Erhardt Library, 2022). The reproducible "Compare and Contrast Informational Texts Graphic Organizer" (page 126) provides a graphic organizer teachers can use with this activity.

Consider the following ideas for using this activity with students.

Idea: Compare and Contrast With a Text

For this exercise, choose two elements of your current lesson you want students to compare and contrast. Find two or more informational texts that provide information about these two topics. Students work in pairs to compare and contrast these texts, exploring their similarities and differences.

Use the following instructions as a template, adjusting as needed for your class.

1. Instruct students to choose a partner.
2. Give each pair a copy of the assigned texts and the "Compare and Contrast Informational Texts Graphic Organizer."
3. Give students ample time to read the articles, compare and contrast them, and complete their graphic organizer.

4. Facilitate a class discussion by inviting pairs to share their findings.
5. Optional: Consider assigning each pair different items to compare and contrast so that the class can cover more content and engage in a high-level discussion in which they exchange more ideas and find opportunities to make connections.

Idea: Compare and Contrast With Research

This variation takes the activity a step further by tasking students with conducting additional research to widen their understanding of competing perspectives on a topic of study.

Use the following instructions as a template, adjusting as needed for your class.

1. Inform students they'll be using the "Compare and Contrast Informational Texts Graphic Organizer" (page 126) they used for the previous exercise.
2. Allow students to work with their partners to seek out additional sources and analyze them alongside their completed graphic organizer.
3. Provide students resources to determine whether their sources are credible.
4. After students complete their graphic organizer and source analysis, give them time to share their graphic organizer and resources with their peers.

Applying research to the Compare and Contrast Informational Texts activity adds complexity to the skill. Students need resources and practice to determine the validity of sources, which is vital in our digital world. When students are able to dive deeply into a topic of their choosing, they are more engaged and motivated to stick with it and learn from it.

Classroom Example

Ms. Hall notices that her students are constantly talking about the latest trends on social media. Some trends she has heard a lot about in her classroom are the various diets that celebrities follow and endorse. She wants to make sure her students have accurate information and are not relying on celebrity endorsements to guide their lifestyle choices.

Ms. Hall builds a lesson for her family and consumer science education class around identifying and understanding relationships using the compare-and-contrast skill. She chooses an article from *Us Weekly* that focuses on celebrity diets and their recommendations for losing weight. Figure 10.3 shows how Ms. Hall designs her lesson plan around this essential skill, including the learning intention and success criteria. To use this template to design your own lesson plan, access the "Planning Lessons Around Essential Skills" reproducible (page 62).

Lesson Plan

Assigned text: "Intermittent Fasting, Plant-Based, Paleo! Celebs Reveal Which Diets Work Best for Them" (Dweck, 2020)

Essential skill: Identify and understand relationships using compare and contrast.

Summary: Students read the article and work to compare and contrast the experts' recommendations.

Grade level: High school

Vigorous learning intention: I can read the article with my partner, compare and contrast the experts' recommendations about the diets mentioned, and complete a personal reflection to discuss with my peers.

Scaffolded success criteria: I know I am successful because

- I can read the article with my partner.
- I can compare source 1 and source 2.
- I can contrast source 1 and source 2.
- I can compare and contrast two of the diets mentioned in the article.
- I can write a personal reflection on what I've learned.

FIGURE 10.3: Ms. Hall's lesson plan for identifying and understanding relationships using compare and contrast.

Ms. Hall instructs students to find a partner. She provides each pair with a copy of the article and graphic organizers. Students work with their partner to read the article and complete the graphic organizer, identifying two expert sources from the article and comparing and contrasting their advice. They work to understand how the sources are the same and how they are different. After students complete their collaborative work, they each return to their desk and take time to write a personal reflection on what they've learned from the exercise. Ms. Hall ends the lesson by facilitating a whole-class discussion and inviting students to share their reflections with their peers. Figure 10.4 (page 124) shows how one student completes their graphic organizer.

Compare and Contrast Informational Texts Graphic Organizer

Instructions: In the space provided, cite two sources you'll use for this activity. Then follow the prompts to compare and contrast the two sources. Where a blank appears, fill in the relevant information. When you're finished, write a personal reflection about what you've discovered.

Cite source 1:
L. Beam, holistic nutrition counselor
Cite source 2:
K. Glassman, registered dietitian and certified dietitian and nutritionist, and J. London, registered dietitian

What do you notice about source 1?	**What do you notice about source 2?**
I researched Laura Beam, the "expert" from the article, and found her on LinkedIn. She has little background in health or nutrition.	I researched Keri Glassman from the article and found her on LinkedIn. She has a master of science degree in dietetics and clinical nutrition services. I researched Jaclyn London from the article, and she is a registered dietitian for Weight Watchers.
One way source 1 and source 2 are similar is . . . Beam, Glassman, and London have interests in helping people to eat healthy.	**One way source 1 and source 2 are different is . . .** Beam is not a registered dietitian; she doesn't have any background in this subject. But Glassman and London have degrees in nutrition and health.
What does source 1 say about intermittent fasting **?** Beam says, "The food you consume should be as nourishing and nutrient-dense as possible" (Dweck, 2020).	**What does source 2 say about** intermittent fasting **?** Glassman says, "In a nutshell, intermittent fasting works. . . . For most people, you're restricting calories and largely cutting out food you shouldn't be eating anyway" (Dweck, 2020).
What does source 1 say about Weight Watchers **?** Nothing	**What does source 2 say about** Weight Watchers **?** London says, "WW helps people adopt healthy habits by setting realistic goals" (Dweck, 2020).
Another way source 1 is similar to source 2 is . . . Beam, Glassman, and London work with celebrities.	**Another way source 1 is different from source 2 is . . .** The article didn't use Beam as an expert for Weight Watchers; instead, the article used a Weight Watchers expert. Why didn't they use an expert for the other diets?

Your reflection of the article:
This article talked about celebrities and their diets. I don't know why anyone would listen to a celebrity and what diet they're on. I think that some celebrities might know something about diets, but only if they do their research. Everybody's body is different. I wouldn't follow a celebrity's diet.

FIGURE 10.4: Sample Compare and Contrast Informational Texts Graphic Organizer.

Compare and Contrast Graphic Organizer

Instructions: In the space provided, write the two items you're comparing and contrasting. In the first box, write two to three sentences describing how these two items are alike. In the second box, use the chart to list the ways these two items differ.

How are they alike?

How are they different?

______________	______________

Compare and Contrast Informational Texts Graphic Organizer

Instructions: In the space provided, cite two sources you'll use for this activity. Then follow the prompts to compare and contrast the two sources. Where a blank appears, fill in the relevant information. When you're finished, write a personal reflection about what you've discovered.

Cite source 1:
Cite source 2:

What do you notice about source 1?	**What do you notice about source 2?**
One way source 1 and source 2 are similar is . . .	**One way source 1 and source 2 are different is . . .**
What does source 1 say about ____________________?	**What does source 2 say about ____________________?**
What does source 1 say about ____________________?	**What does source 2 say about ____________________?**
Another way source 1 is similar to source 2 is . . .	**Another way source 1 is different from source 2 is . . .**

Your reflection of the article:

CHAPTER 11

DELINEATE AND EVALUATE ARGUMENTS

When students are asked to delineate an argument, they must be able to describe, portray, or set forth that argument with accuracy and detail. Students may not think of the word *argument* in that context; rather, they may have the connotation of bickering or fighting. When teaching this skill, make sure students understand that *argument* means a "coherent series of reasons, statements, or facts intended to support or establish a point of view" (Argument, n.d.). In evaluating an argument, students should be able to assess its quality and judge whether the argument fulfills its purpose—to urge a person to believe the argument based on the reasons given. If the argument is a poor one, it won't encourage the listener to believe the conclusion based on the reasons given.

When students are able to delineate and evaluate arguments—an essential skill central to their civic and academic lives—they become better citizens and better consumers of information. According to Odell Education (2020), "Citizens have access to a glut of information (some of which is nothing more than opinion passed off as fact) and are often bombarded by bombast rather than engaged in reasoned and civil debate" (p. 2). Now more than ever in a society with easy access to social media and rampant misinformation, students need to be adept at spotting misleading or false statements and deceptive reasoning. Every day, in every classroom, students are expected to understand and analyze arguments. However, this work requires students to possess and practice explicit communication skills that some have not adequately developed. Scholars Patricia Armstrong, Sonja Moyer, and Katherine Stanton (n.d.) write, "It is only through this critical evaluation that students can distinguish among competing claims for truth and determine which arguments and points of views they can trust and those of which they should be skeptical." To be successful 21st century learners and professionals, students must be able to understand that not all information is reliable, determine credible sources, conduct research, and think critically about texts. Delineating and evaluating arguments is a vital skill students require in academics and beyond.

This chapter offers two activities students can use to learn how to delineate and evaluate arguments. These activities are also appropriate for students who have already encountered this skill but need to practice it. Each activity includes two ideas for using the activity with students as well as a classroom example, a sample lesson plan, and reproducibles.

Activity: Language of Learning

This activity provides students with specific questions to determine the credibility of research sources. Skilled and motivated writers can easily write compelling arguments that aren't true or aren't published with the reader's best interests in mind. Teacher mentor Amie Weinberg (2022) notes, "There are many platforms (like GoDaddy and Wix) that allow individuals to easily create professional-quality websites without having to learn HTML coding. That means that anyone with internet access can publish virtually anything on the internet," which, of course, makes determining the validity of a site more difficult.

When students can't determine what is authentic versus what is fake, the consequences can be alarming. A research study conducted by the Stanford Graduate School of Education (2021) found a "woeful inability by high schoolers to detect fake news on the internet suggests an urgent need for schools to integrate new tools and curriculum into classrooms that boost students' digital skills." Students are tasked with researching various topics in all their content areas; to do this successfully, they need the skills to discern fact from fiction and evidence from opinion. Teachers must provide students the tools to help them forge opinions and points of view that are based on real, accurate information.

The Language of Learning gives students targeted language that helps them distinguish between credible and fraudulent sources. As a result, I recommend using this activity as you introduce students to this essential skill. It provides a scaffolded approach to the success criteria and walks students through explicit questions designed to help them become savvy consumers of information. Make sure to model this skill with students to ensure they understand the concept and the process.

In this activity, students inspect various data without context and analyze the sources to determine whether they are credible. When introducing this skill, illustrate the difference between credible sources and opinions, as students need explicit teaching and practice to recognize the difference and understand why it matters. The reproducible "Language of Learning Chart" (page 138) contains a tool teachers can provide students for working with this activity.

Consider the following ideas for using this activity with students.

Idea: Determine Fact or Fiction

In this version of the activity, present students with data you've gathered on the topic of an upcoming lesson. Gather data from a variety of sources, some credible and others not (these may be in the form of graphs, quotes, charts, or similar forms). It's particularly hard to gauge the validity of data when they appear without context. Present the data to students without commentary or context, and task them with determining the source and analyzing whether it's credible. Then host a class discussion about the process itself, uncovering and highlighting what clues students should use to determine credibility.

Use the following instructions as a template, adjusting as needed for your class.

1. Gather data from a variety of sources with conflicting messages about your topic of study, and post them around the room.
2. Instruct students to complete a gallery walk and inspect the sources.
3. Break students into groups, and provide them with the "Language of Learning Chart." Students use the organizer to help them determine which data are credible and which are not.
4. Host a class discussion in which groups share their findings and discuss what made the process confusing, what tools helped them determine credibility, and what they'll do differently when engaging with arguments in the future.

Idea: Create a Personalized Graph

For this more challenging version of the activity, students create their own graph, table, or pie chart. They may work with whatever topic you assign or with one of their choice in alignment with the current lesson. In completing this activity, students notice how context plays a key role in communicating accurate information to the reader.

Use the following instructions as a template, adjusting as needed for your class.

1. Allow students to work in pairs.
2. Instruct student pairs to utilize research focused on their topic to create a graph, table, or pie chart that represents data.
3. Have each student pair draft an argument reflecting the data in their graph, table, or pie chart.
4. Have each pair present their argument to the class and explain what their argument is; how they constructed their graph, table, or chart; and why the context matters for accurately representing the facts to the reader.

Classroom Example

Mr. Wilson decides to share with his students statistics on teen behaviors. His students have strong opinions regarding the information on the graph he presents. Many students are trying to make arguments about the information; however, their arguments are poorly constructed and ineffective. As a result of their limited ability to argue and evaluate arguments, Mr. Wilson constructs a lesson around the skill of delineating and evaluating arguments.

Figure 11.1 shows how Mr. Wilson designs his lesson plan around this essential skill, including the learning intention and success criteria. To use this template to design your own lesson plan, access the "Planning Lessons Around Essential Skills" reproducible (page 62).

Lesson Plan

Assigned text: "What's Going On in This Graph? | Teen Behaviors" (The Learning Network, 2022)

Essential skill: Delineate and evaluate arguments.

Summary: Students focus on how to read a graph, concentrating on describing and evaluating their argument and those of their peers regarding the information reflected in the graph.

Grade level: High school

Vigorous learning intention: I can read the graph, predict trends based on the graph information, and research those trends to describe and evaluate my argument and those of my peers based on the graph information.

Scaffolded success criteria: I know I am successful because

- I can read the graph.
- Based on the graph, I can predict trends.
- I can research those trends to determine whether my predictions were accurate.
- I can describe those trends to my peers.
- I can evaluate the arguments presented by my peers.

FIGURE 11.1: Mr. Wilson's lesson plan for delineating and evaluating arguments.

Mr. Wilson divides students into groups of three, assigns each group a graph, and instructs groups to analyze their graph and give their predictions about the whys and hows of future trends. At the end of class, students reflect on the discussion by starting to fill in the "Language of Learning Chart" (page 138). On another day during the unit, Mr. Wilson tasks students with revisiting their notes and researching the trends they identified. Students participate in a class discussion, presenting evidence, justifying predictions, and evaluating their peers' arguments.

Figure 11.2 (page 132) shows how one student completes the "Language of Learning Chart."

Language of Learning Chart

Instructions: Write the success criteria for this lesson in the first column. In the second column, explain how you applied those criteria during the activity. In the final column, write your reflections in response to the prompts in the Language of Learning column.

Scaffolded Success Criteria	Application	Language of Learning	My Reflection
I can read the graph.	It looks like cigarette use, alcohol use, and marijuana use are going down. Teens aren't watching TV as much as they were in 1989. But the use of devices is way up. Also, teens feel sad, and many have considered suicide.	**"Who, what, where, when, and why? How?"** **"What do I think?"**	The graph is about teen behaviors. Overall, it's good that cigarette use, alcohol use, and marijuana use are down. But devices are up and so are suicides. I wonder if the use of devices and suicides are connected.
Based on the graph, I can predict trends.	I think the use of devices will only continue to go up. Also, I think teens will continue to feel sad because we are under a lot of pressure. Social media doesn't help teens feel better about themselves.	**"This is an example of . . ."** **"This is important because . . ."**	This is important because I think these things are connected. We will spend more time on devices, and teens will be on social media where other teens can hurt their feelings.
I can research those trends to determine whether my predictions were accurate.	I found this quote on Newswise (Brigham Young University, 2021): "'Research shows that girls and women in general are very relationally attuned and sensitive to interpersonal stressors, and social media is all about relationships,' Coyne explained. 'At 13, girls are just starting to be ready to handle the darker underbelly of social media, such as FOMO (fear of missing out), constant comparisons and cyberbullying. A 13-year-old is probably not developmentally ready for three hours of social media a day.'"	**"What is the purpose?"** **"What is important in this information? Why?"** **"What crucial information are we missing?"** **"What are the underlying assumptions of the author's message?"** **"Why should I know about this?"**	This is important because it explains that girls and women are more susceptible to FOMO, comparisons, and cyberbullying. I should know about this so I'm careful about social media, and it's important not to let it run my life.

I can describe those trends to my peers.	I agree with these trends because I see them with my friends; they're on social media all the time, and many of them just seem sad. I explained these trends to my friends, and several of them agreed.	**"Based on the evidence, we must conclude . . ."** **"The most logical conclusion we can draw from this evidence is . . ."** **"The reason this is reasonable is . . ."**	Based on the graph and what I see and my own research from Newswise, I conclude that this evidence is accurate.
I can evaluate the arguments presented by my peers.	One of my peers found research from CNN Health. CNN is a trusted news source. Also, the quote came from an expert in the field, so I believe this source and I concur with their argument.	**"I agree with this because . . ."** **"I disagree because . . ."** **"A better solution would be . . ."** **"The facts that are most important are . . ."**	I agree with this argument because I'm online a lot and I know my friends are, too. The facts that are shown in this article are important because I think being online too much is not positive. Maybe a better solution would be to limit my own screen time; go for a walk or try to put the computer away.

FIGURE 11.2: Sample Language of Learning Chart.

Activity: Evidence Gathering

In this activity, students have the chance to determine whether their opinion is indeed accurate. We all have our opinions, but how do we know we're right? Is there research to support our opinions, or have we cultivated them based on personal feelings or peer pressure? According to journalist and teacher Esther Wojcicki (2021), "Learning to distinguish fact and opinion is one of the most important skills students can learn in school. It serves students for a lifetime and in all aspects of life—from knowing how advertisers get them to buy products to analyzing news stories and the sources."

When students know how to analyze their own opinions and ensure they align with facts, they gain confidence and integrity. Furthermore, they are able to defend their opinions with credible evidence and argue persuasively with facts.

Conversely, if students do not master this essential skill, it "has a negative impact on [their] country and on their own lives" because students will rely on someone's hearsay to make an argument (Wojcicki, 2021). Therefore, students must practice this skill to learn to create opinions that are based on facts, not emotions or sentiment. This activity provides students the opportunity to begin with their opinion on a topic and to explore the research on that topic to discover whether the evidence supports or refutes their opinion. The reproducible "Evidence Gathering Worksheet" (page 140) contains a worksheet teachers can provide students for working with this activity.

Consider the following ideas for using this activity with students.

Idea: Read What the Experts Say

This activity is ideal when introducing a film genre, art movement, music movement, or other subjective area of study because students can form their own opinion and conduct research to support or refute it. To support students in delineating and evaluating their argument or the argument of a peer, encourage students to read expert accounts of the content.

Use the following instructions as a template, adjusting as needed for your class.

1. Assign students to work in pairs with the content of the lesson (a text, film, song, piece of music, or other subjective media).
2. Provide each pair a copy of the "Evidence Gathering Worksheet."

3. Instruct students to write their opinion of the content and then conduct research to identify expert analysis on the subject.
4. Task students with completing the worksheet by evaluating their opinion against the expert analysis.
5. Facilitate a whole-class discussion, inviting students to share their findings.

Idea: Gather Evidence

Consider scaffolding this lesson by giving students a chance to debate a topic of their choice. We know "student choice enhances students' excitement about topics, curriculum, and their interests" (Kiser, 2020). When students have choice, they are more interested in the topic and more likely to stick with it. However, be selective about the topic to keep student discussion school appropriate.

Use the following instructions as a template, adjusting as needed for your class.

1. Have students select a topic related to the current lesson and write a thesis statement that states their opinion on the topic.
2. Provide each student with the "Evidence Gathering Worksheet" (page 140).
3. Allow time for students to conduct research to identify expert analysis on the subject.
4. Task students with completing the worksheet by evaluating their opinion against the expert analysis.
5. Host a class discussion, inviting students to share their reflection on the process. Ask questions such as these: "Were you surprised by what you discovered? What factors shaped your opinion? Did you change your opinion based on expert analysis?"

Classroom Example

When Ms. Garam asks for her students' opinions regarding a piece of art, she notices they offer opinions based on what they see because their prior knowledge about the art and artist is limited. Ms. Garam decides to build a lesson for her art class around the essential skill of delineating and evaluating arguments. She wants her students to research the artist and the art to learn more about the work so they can offer justification for their opinion. She hopes the exercise will empower students to describe the art accurately and state reasons and facts that establish their assessment of the art rather than express whether they like the piece or think it's appealing.

Figure 11.3 shows how she designs her lesson plan around this essential skill, including the learning intention and success criteria. To use this template to design your own lesson plan, access the "Planning Lessons Around Essential Skills" reproducible (page 62).

Lesson Plan

Assigned text: *The Scream* (Munch, 1893)

Essential skill: Delineate and evaluate arguments.

Summary: Student pairs analyze Edvard Munch's *The Scream*, state their opinion of the painting, and use research to justify their evaluation and defend their critique.

Grade level: Middle school

Vigorous learning intention: I can give my opinion of a painting, analyze the painting with the support of art experts, justify or alter my evaluation, and write a brief summary.

Scaffolded success criteria: I know I am successful because

- I can give my opinion of the painting.
- I can research the painting and access expert analysis.
- I can describe my argument utilizing the expert analysis and share it with my peers.
- I can evaluate a peer's argument.

FIGURE 11.3: Ms. Garam's lesson plan for delineating and evaluating arguments.

Ms. Garam assigns students to work with a partner to view Munch's *The Scream* and form an opinion of the painting. She provides each student with a worksheet and resources for researching expert analysis of the painting. Students record their opinion on their worksheet, research what experts say about the painting, and search for evidence that supports or refutes their opinion. Finally, students evaluate their argument in light of the research they've encountered. Ms. Garam concludes the lesson by facilitating a classroom discussion, inviting students to share their opinions and how those opinions changed as a result of the expert arguments they encountered.

Figure 11.4 shows how one student completes the worksheet.

Evidence Gathering Worksheet

Instructions: Read the following statements, and write your responses.

Topic or unit: Expressionism

Don't forget to use your vocabulary terms wherever you can as you write your responses.

In my opinion:

Edvard Munch's *The Scream* is my favorite painting because it is an iconic piece of art that everyone can relate to since the agonized face in the painting is a symbol of the anxiety of the human condition.

I can delineate or describe this artwork**:**

It shows the sadness of humankind, and the figure's face exemplifies fear. In the painting, there is an abstracted figure standing while covering their ears, evoking the expression of fear and anguish, set against a swirling and moving background of densely saturated complementary hues.

I believe *The Scream* **is important or not important because:**

Important because it's an example of the symbolist movement as well as inspiration for the expressionist movement of the early 20th century. Expressionist artists expressed their inner emotions, fantasies, or thoughts independent from reality.

I can evaluate my argument about this artwork **based on the following evidence:**

I am able to find art experts who agree. "Described by Oslo's Munch Museum as 'the actual mental image of the existential angst of civilized man,' *The Scream* is dominated by feelings of anxiety and alienation that were often associated with modern life at the turn of the century" (Annenberg Learner, n.d.).

Using the preceding items, I can justify or refute my initial opinion:

Edvard Munch's *The Scream* is my favorite painting. It shows the sadness of humankind, and the figure's face exemplifies fear. In the painting, there is an abstracted figure standing while covering their ears, evoking the expression of fear and anguish, set against a swirling and moving background of densely saturated complementary hues.

The Scream is an iconic piece of art that everyone can relate to since the agonized face in the painting is a symbol of the anxiety of the human condition.

The Scream is important because it's an example of the symbolist movement as well as an important inspiration for the expressionist movement of the early 20th century.

According to Annenberg Learner (n.d.) and Oslo's Munch Museum, *The Scream* is the "'actual mental image of the existential angst of civilized man,' . . . dominated by feelings of anxiety and alienation that were often associated with modern life at the turn of the century."

FIGURE 11.4: Sample Evidence Gathering Worksheet.

Language of Learning Chart

Instructions: Write the success criteria for this lesson in the first column. In the second column, explain how you applied those criteria during the activity. In the final column, write your reflections in response to the prompts in the Language of Learning column.

Scaffolded Success Criteria	Application	Language of Learning	My Reflection
		"Who, what, where, when, and why? How?" **"What do I think?"**	
		"This is an example of . . ." **"This is important because . . ."**	

Scaffolded Success Criteria	Application	Language of Learning	My Reflection
		"What is the purpose?" "What is important in this information? Why?" "What crucial information are we missing?" "What are the underlying assumptions of the author's message?" "Why should I know about this?"	
		"Based on the evidence, we must conclude . . ." "The most logical conclusion we can draw from this evidence is . . ." "The reason this is reasonable is . . ."	
		"I agree with this because . . ." "I disagree because . . ." "A better solution would be . . ." "The facts that are most important are . . ."	

page 2 of 2

Evidence Gathering Worksheet

Instructions: Read the following statements, and write your responses.

Topic or unit: ____________________ *Don't forget to use your vocabulary terms wherever you can as you write your responses.*
In my opinion:
I can delineate or describe this ____________________:
I believe ____________________ is important or not important because:
I can evaluate my argument about this ____________________ based on the following evidence:
Using the preceding items, I can justify or refute my initial opinion:

EPILOGUE

In writing this book, I wanted to provide teachers, paraprofessionals, classroom aides, and coaches—all educators—the opportunity to teach essential literacy skills that are easily transferable beyond the classroom walls. I wanted to equip them with the tools to clear the path for students who face educational barriers due to underdeveloped skills. Students' success in K–12 classrooms and the workforce depends on their ability to master these skills and transfer them to diverse contexts.

As I was writing this book and researching essential skills, I realized that we educators, regardless of the grade level or content area we work with, encounter these skills in our classrooms—often without realizing it. This book aims to make that teaching of essential skills explicit. I hope you see your classroom culture, instruction, and teaching techniques with new eyes as a result of what you've read.

Now that you've come to the end of the book, I trust you have developed a foundational understanding of essential skills, why they are so valuable and purposeful, and why every teacher should intentionally teach them. You know how to nurture a classroom culture that supports the implementation of these skills, how to unpack your state's or province's standards to plan lessons around the skills, and how to use brain-based teaching techniques to support students to move toward mastery. I hope with the tools you encountered in part 2 (page 49), you will be empowered to customize lessons to suit your grade level, your content area, and your students' unique needs.

Thank you for sharing this journey with me as we continue to offer students the very best of ourselves as teachers and fellow learners. I look forward to many more opportunities to teach and learn with you.

REFERENCES AND RESOURCES

ACT. (n.d.). *ACT college and career readiness standards*. Accessed at www.act.org/content/act/en/college-and-career-readiness/standards.html on October 7, 2022.

Ahlberg, J., & Ahlberg, A. (1986). *The jolly postman: Or other people's letters*. Boston: Little, Brown.

Akolo, W. (2022, January 25). *Comparing and contrasting: A guide to improve your essays*. Accessed at https://prowritingaid.com/comparing-contrasting on January 24, 2023.

Allen, J. (2008). *More tools for teaching content literacy*. Portland, ME: Stenhouse.

Amaro, M. (n.d.). *Why teacher expectations are important for student achievement*. Accessed at https://thehighlyeffectiveteacher.com/why-teacher-expectations-are-important-for-student-achievement on October 6, 2022.

Anderson, A. R., Christenson, S. L., Sinclair, M. F., & Lehr, C. A. (2004). Check & Connect: The importance of relationships for promoting engagement with school. *Journal of School Psychology*, *42*(2), 95–113.

Andrew, S. (2022, August 6). *The last Salem witch has been exonerated, thanks to an eighth-grade teacher and her students*. Accessed at www.cnn.com/2022/08/06/us/salem-witch-trials-exonerated-elizabeth-johnson-cec/index.html on October 7, 2022.

Annenberg Learner. (n.d.). *Art: The scream*. Accessed at www.learner.org/series/art-through-time-a-global-view/dreams-and-visions/the-scream on October 7, 2022.

Argument. (n.d.). In *Merriam-Webster's online dictionary*. Accessed at www.merriam-webster.com/dictionary/argument on January 1, 2023.

Armstrong, P., Moyer, S., & Stanton, K. (n.d.). *Learning to analyze and critically evaluate ideas, arguments, and points of view*. Accessed at www.ideaedu.org/idea-notes-on-learning/learning-to-analyze-and-critically-evaluate-ideas-arguments-and-points-of-view on October 7, 2022.

Baker, G., Kulesa, A. C., & Schwartze, L. (2019, September). *Unfinished: Insights from ongoing work to accelerate outcomes for students with learning gaps*. Sudbury, MA: Bellwether Education Partners. Accessed at https://bellwether.org/publications/unfinished-insights-ongoing-work-accelerate-outcomes-students-learning-gaps on October 6, 2022.

Barnett, S. M., & Ceci, S. J. (2002). When and where do we apply what we learn? A taxonomy for far transfer. *Psychological Bulletin*, *128*(4), 612–637.

Beck, H. (2021). *Scatterbrain: How the mind's mistakes make humans creative, innovative, and successful* (B. L. Crook, Trans.). Vancouver, British Columbia, Canada: Greystone Books.

Beers, K. (2003). *When kids can't read, what teachers can do: A guide for teachers, 6–12.* Portsmouth, NH: Heinemann.

Beers, K. [@kylenebeers]. (2018, April 11). *THE best summarizing strategy I've ever seen: Somebody Wanted But So* [Image attached] [Tweet]. Twitter. Accessed at https://twitter.com/kylenebeers/status/984046897848573952? on January 26, 2023.

Beers, K., & Probst, R. E. (2016). *Reading nonfiction: Notice and note stances, signposts, and strategies.* Portsmouth, NH: Heinemann.

Belafi, C., Hwa, Y.-Y., & Kaffenberger, M. (2020). *Building on solid foundations: Prioritising universal, early, conceptual and procedural mastery of foundational skills.* Oxford, England: Research on Improving Systems of Education. Accessed at https://riseprogramme.org/sites/default/files/2020-11/RISE%20Insight_2020_21_Belafi_Hwa_Kaffenberger.pdf on October 24, 2022.

Brabeck, M., Jeffrey, J., & Fry, S. (2015). *Practice for knowledge acquisition (not drill and kill).* Accessed at www.apa.org/education-career/k12/practice-acquisition on October 7, 2022.

Brautigan, R. (1971). The Scarlatti tilt. In *Revenge of the lawn: Stories, 1962–1970* (p. 50). New York: Simon & Schuster.

Brigham Young University. (2021, February 9). *10-year study shows elevated suicide risk from excess social media time for teen girls.* Accessed at www.newswise.com/articles/10-year-study-shows-elevated-suicide-risk-from-excess-social-media-time-for-teen-girls on October 7, 2022.

Brooks, K. J. (2020, October 7). *ACT and SAT scores no longer required for admissions at some colleges.* Accessed at www.cbsnews.com/news/act-and-sat-no-longer-required-college-admissions on October 6, 2022.

Brown, M. D. (n.d.). *Cause-and-effect writing challenges students.* Accessed at www.educationworld.com/a_curr/curr376b.shtml on December 27, 2022.

Buehl, D. (2017). *Classroom strategies for interactive learning* (4th ed.). Portsmouth, NH: Stenhouse.

Buffum, A., Mattos, M., & Malone, J. (2018). *Taking action: A handbook for RTI at Work.* Bloomington, IN: Solution Tree Press.

Burnett, C. (2017, February 16). *Engage your child with informational reading* [Blog post]. Accessed at www.scholastic.com/parents/books-and-reading/raise-a-reader-blog/engage-your-child-informational-reading.html on December 31, 2022.

Burns, L. (2022, February 3). *How and why to teach your students to compare and contrast* [Blog post]. Accessed at www.hopeineducation.com/blog/081-how-and-why-to-teach-your-students-to-compare-and-contrast on October 7, 2022.

Burns, M. K., Sarlo, R., & Pettersson, H. (n.d.). *Response to intervention for literacy in secondary schools.* Accessed at www.rtinetwork.org/learn/rti-in-secondary-schools/rti-literacy-secondary-schools on October 6, 2022.

Caine, R. N., & Caine, G. (1991). *Making connections: Teaching and the human brain.* Alexandria, VA: ASCD.

California Department of Education. (2013). *California Common Core State Standards: English language arts and literacy in history/social studies, science, and technical subjects.* Sacramento, CA: Author. Accessed at www.cde.ca.gov/be/st/ss/documents/finalelaccssstandards.pdf on October 6, 2022.

California State Board of Education. (2022, July 13). *Content standards.* Accessed at www.cde.ca.gov/be/st/ss on December 15, 2022.

Chapman University. (2016, March 28). *Expressionism: An artistic movement and an art term?* [Blog post]. Accessed at https://blogs.chapman.edu/collections/2016/03/28/expressionism on October 7, 2022.

Children's Reading Foundation. (n.d.). *Third grade reading success matters.* Accessed at www.readingfoundation.org/third-grade-reading-matters on October 7, 2022.

Clark-Robinson, M. (2018). *Let the children march* (F. Morrison, Illus.). Boston: Houghton Mifflin Harcourt.

Common Core State Standards Initiative. (n.d.). *About the standards.* Accessed at www.corestandards.org/about-the-standards on October 6, 2022.

Cursino, M. (2022, July 11). *Yosemite's giant sequoias: Wildfire threatens world's largest trees.* Accessed at www.bbc.com/news/world-us-canada-62117139 on October 7, 2022.

Dabell, J. (2021, August 26). *The Frayer model.* Accessed at https://johndabell.com/2021/08/26/the-frayer-model on December 25, 2022.

Darling-Hammond, L., Flook, L., Cook-Harvey, C., Barron, B., & Osher, D. (2020). Implications for educational practice of the science of learning and development. *Applied Developmental Science, 24*(2). Accessed at www.tandfonline.com/doi/full/10.1080/10888691.2018.1537791 on October 6, 2022.

Davies, R. (n.d.). *How to effectively teach compare and contrast using a mentor text.* Accessed at www.differentiatedteaching.com/compare-and-contrast on October 7, 2022.

Decker, D. M., Dona, D. P., & Christenson, S. L. (2007). Behaviorally at-risk African American students: The importance of student-teacher relationships for student outcomes. *Journal of School Psychology, 45*(1), 83–109.

Delineate. (n.d.). In *Merriam-Webster's online dictionary.* Accessed at www.merriam-webster.com/dictionary/delineate on January 1, 2023.

Dodge, J. (2009). *25 quick formative assessments for a differentiated classroom: Easy, low-prep assessments that help you pinpoint students' needs and reach all learners.* New York: Scholastic.

Dweck, S. (2020, January 1). *Intermittent fasting, plant-based, paleo! Celebs reveal which diets work best for them.* Accessed at www.usmagazine.com/celebrity-body/pictures/celebrities-reveal-which-diets-work-best-for-them on October 7, 2022.

Eberly Center. (n.d.a). *Students are confused, bored, or frustrated with the course.* Accessed at www.cmu.edu/teaching/solveproblem/strat-behaverudely/behaverudely-03.html on January 26, 2023.

Eberly Center. (n.d.b). *Students have learned the individual skill or piece of knowledge but can't apply it in complex contexts because they haven't practiced the skills of integration and synthesis.* Accessed at www.cmu.edu/teaching/solveproblem/strat-cantapply/cantapply-03.html on October 6, 2022.

Egger, F., Conzelmann, A., & Schmidt, M. (2018). The effect of acute cognitively engaging physical activity breaks on children's executive functions: Too much of a good thing? *Psychology of Sport and Exercise, 36*, 178–186.

Elsevier. (2017, October 5). *How much can watching hockey stress your heart?* Accessed at www.sciencedaily.com/releases/2017/10/171005102717.htm on October 6, 2022.

Ewing Marion Kauffman Foundation. (2019). *Visions of the future.* Accessed at www.kauffman.org/wp-content/uploads/2019/09/Visions-of-the-Future_v3.pdf on October 6, 2022.

Farmer, G. (2020, August 6). *How schools and teachers can get better at cultural competence* [Blog post]. Accessed at www.educationnext.org/how-schools-teachers-can-get-better-cultural-competence on December 15, 2022.

Ferlazzo, L. (2020, June 15). *The whys and hows of activating students' background knowledge* [Blog post]. Accessed at www.edweek.org/teaching-learning/opinion-the-whys-hows-of-activating-students-background-knowledge/2020/06 on October 6, 2022.

Florida National University. (2019, August 13). *The benefits of studying with music*. Accessed at www.fnu.edu/benefits-studying-music on October 6, 2022.

Fogg, N., Harrington, P., & Khatiwada, I. (2019). *Skills and the earnings of college graduates*. Princeton, NJ: Educational Testing Service.

Frayer, D. A., Fredrick, W. C., & Klausmeier, H. J. (1969). *A schema for testing the level of concept mastery* (Technical Report No. 16). Madison, WI: Wisconsin Research and Development Center for Cognitive Learning.

Galley, M. (2020, August 31). *Why cause-and-effect thinking is important* [Blog post]. Accessed at https://blog.thinkreliability.com/why-cause-and-effect-thinking-is-important on December 27, 2022.

Glossary of Education Reform. (2015, April 6). *Scaffolding*. Accessed at www.edglossary.org/scaffolding on December 15, 2022.

Gonser, S. (2022, June 10). *6 quick strategies to build vocabulary*. Accessed at www.edutopia.org/article/6-quick-strategies-build-vocabulary on December 25, 2022.

Gonzalez, J. (2014, April 14). *How we pronounce student names, and why it matters*. Accessed at www.cultofpedagogy.com/gift-of-pronunciation on October 6, 2022.

Grafwallner, P. (2017a, November 2). *Keeping learning real, relevant, and relatable*. Accessed at www.edutopia.org/article/keeping-learning-real-relevant-and-relatable on December 14, 2022.

Grafwallner, P. (2017b, December 19). *What I've learned from special ed teachers*. Accessed at www.edutopia.org/article/what-ive-learned-special-ed-teachers on October 6, 2022.

Grafwallner, P. (2019, April 18). *A framework for lesson planning*. Accessed at www.edutopia.org/article/framework-lesson-planning on October 6, 2022.

Grafwallner, P. (2020). *Ready to learn: The FRAME model for optimizing student success*. Bloomington, IN: Solution Tree Press.

Grafwallner, P. (2021). *Not yet . . . and that's OK: How productive struggle fosters student learning*. Bloomington, IN: Solution Tree Press.

Haberland, N., & Abuya, T. (2021, May 10). *What the COVID-19 pandemic is showing us about the global learning crisis* [Blog post]. Accessed at www.cfr.org/blog/what-covid-19-pandemic-showing-us-about-global-learning-crisis on November 8, 2022.

Hammond, Z. (2015). *Culturally responsive teaching and the brain: Promoting authentic engagement and rigor among culturally and linguistically diverse students*. Thousand Oaks, CA: Corwin Press.

Harlacher, J. E., & Whitcomb, S. A. (2022). *Bolstering student resilience: Creating a classroom with consistency, connection, and compassion*. Bloomington, IN: Marzano Resources.

Hart, L. A. (1983). *Human brain and human learning*. New York: Longman.

Hauth, A. (2019, April 16). *Need help learning a new word? Sketch it!* [Blog post]. Accessed at www.readnaturally.com/about-us/blog/need-help-learning-a-new-word-sketch-it on December 25, 2022.

Helman, L. (2014, May 22). *Building academic vocabulary and concepts, brick by brick*. Accessed at www.ascd.org/el/articles/building-academic-vocabulary-and-concepts-brick-by-brick on October 6, 2022.

Helmenstine, A. M. (2019, January 19). *Why is chemistry so hard?* Accessed at www.thoughtco.com/why-is-chemistry-so-hard-604145 on December 25, 2022.

Herbert, A., Saavedra, J., Marr, L., & Jenkins, R. (2021, November 4). *The urgent need to focus on foundational skills* [Blog post]. Accessed at https://blogs.worldbank.org/education/urgent-need-focus-foundational-skills on October 5, 2022.

Homer. (1999). *The odyssey* (R. Fagles, Trans.). New York: Penguin Classics. (Original work published in English 1614)

Hsu, J. L., & Goldsmith, G. R. (2021). Instructor strategies to alleviate stress and anxiety among college and university STEM students. *CBE: Life Sciences Education, 20*(1), es1. Accessed at www.ncbi.nlm.nih.gov/pmc/articles/PMC8108494 on October 5, 2022.

Indeed Editorial Team. (2022a, September 20). *Cause and effect analysis: Definition, benefits and use.* Accessed at www.indeed.com/career-advice/career-development/cause-and-effect-analysis on December 28, 2022.

Indeed Editorial Team. (2022b, March 25). *Making inferences: How to build this critical thinking skill.* Accessed at www.indeed.com/career-advice/career-development/making-inferences on October 7, 2022.

Indiana Department of Education. (2020). *Indiana academic standards English language arts*. Indianapolis, IN: Author. Accessed at www.in.gov/sboe/files/ELA-Standards-2020.pdf on October 7, 2022.

Individuals With Disabilities Education Improvement Act of 2004, Pub. L. No. 108-446 § 300.115 (2004).

Jandhyala, D. (2017, December 8). *Visual learning: 6 reasons why visuals are the most powerful aspect of elearning.* Accessed at https://elearningindustry.com/visual-learning-6-reasons-visuals-powerful-aspect-elearning on October 7, 2022.

Jarzabek, B. (2019, May 14). *A teacher's tip: Want to foster a love of reading? Let students pick their own books. Giving my kids voice and choice changed my classroom.* Accessed at www.the74million.org/article/a-teachers-tip-want-to-foster-a-love-of-reading-in-students-let-them-pick-their-own-books-how-voice-and-choice-has-changed-my-classroom on December 14, 2022.

Jensen, E. (2008). *Brain-based learning: The new paradigm of teaching* (2nd ed.). Thousand Oaks, CA: Corwin Press.

Jensen, E. (2010). *Jensen learning guide to brain-based teaching.* Maunaloa, HI: Jensen Learning. Accessed at https://ventana.fl.unc.edu.ar/files/movement-the-brain.pdf on October 6, 2022.

Johns Hopkins Medicine. (n.d.). *Intermittent fasting: What is it, and how does it work?* Accessed at www.hopkinsmedicine.org/health/wellness-and-prevention/intermittent-fasting-what-is-it-and-how-does-it-work on December 17, 2022.

Johnson, E. (n.d.). *How to develop an effective Tier 2 system.* Accessed at www.rtinetwork.org/essential/tieredinstruction/tier2/how-to-develop-an-effective-tier-2-system on October 5, 2022.

Kessels, U., & Heyder, A. (2020). Not stupid, but lazy? Psychological benefits of disruptive classroom behavior from an attributional perspective. *Social Psychology of Education, 23*(3), 583–613. https://doi.org/10.1007/s11218-020-09550-6

Khillar, S. (2021, July 19). *Difference between TikTok and Instagram.* Accessed at www.differencebetween.net/technology/difference-between-tiktok-and-instagram on October 6, 2022.

King, M. L., Jr. (1963, August). *Letter from Birmingham jail.* Accessed at www.csuchico.edu/iege/_assets/documents/susi-letter-from-birmingham-jail.pdf on December 15, 2022.

Kiser, S. (2020, December 17). *The benefits of student choice.* Accessed at www.teachhub.com/professional-development/2020/12/the-benefits-of-student-choice on January 2, 2023.

Kittinger, J. S. (2010). *Rosa's bus: The ride to civil rights* (S. Walker, Illus.). Honesdale, PA: Calkins Creek.

Klein, A. (2019, September 24). *Teens feel ready for college, but not so much for work.* Accessed at www.edweek.org/teaching-learning/teens-feel-ready-for-college-but-not-so-much-for-work/2019/09 on October 6, 2022.

Lambert, K. (n.d.). *"It's just my opinion" and the burden of proof.* Accessed at www.educationworld.com/teachers/its-just-my-opinion-and-burden-proof on October 7, 2022.

Lawson, A. P., & Mayer, R. E. (2021). Benefits of writing an explanation during pauses in multimedia lessons. *Educational Psychology Review, 33*(4), 1859–1885. https://doi.org/10.1007/s10648-021-09594-w

The Learning Network. (2022, May 5). What's going on in this graph? | Teen behaviors. *The New York Times.* Accessed at www.nytimes.com/2022/05/05/learning/whats-going-on-in-this-graph-may-11-2022.html on January 2, 2023.

Lee, J. (2021, August 5). *States are implementing new educational standards, signaling the end of Common Core.* Accessed at www.cnbc.com/2021/08/05/states-are-implementing-new-educational-standards-signaling-the-end-of-common-core.html on October 6, 2022.

Let's Talk Science. (n.d.). *Comparing and contrasting.* Accessed at https://letstalkscience.ca/educational-resources/learning-strategies/comparing-contrasting on December 30, 2022.

Levine, S. (2022, March 20). *Contrasting cases: A simple strategy for deep understanding.* Accessed at www.cultofpedagogy.com/contrasting-cases on December 31, 2022.

Literacy. (n.d.). In *Merriam-Webster's online dictionary.* Accessed at www.merriam-webster.com/dictionary/literacy on October 7, 2022.

Luhby, T. (2022, September 7). *Fewer children faced food insecurity last year, but more elderly Americans did.* Accessed at www.cnn.com/2022/09/07/politics/food-insecurity-children-elderly/index.html on December 14, 2022.

Lumen Learning. (n.d.). *Main idea, purpose, and audience.* Accessed at https://courses.lumenlearning.com/suny-esc-introtocollegereadingandwriting/chapter/analyzing-the-main-idea on December 19, 2022.

Lynch, M. (2020, June 18). *Why students struggle with reading comprehension.* Accessed at www.theedadvocate.org/why-students-struggle-with-reading-comprehension on December 15, 2022.

Mac Donnchaidh, S. (n.d.a). *Identifying the main idea of the story: A guide for students and teachers.* Accessed at https://literacyideas.com/getting-the-main-idea on December 19, 2022.

Mac Donnchaidh, S. (n.d.b). *Teaching cause and effect in reading and writing.* Accessed at https://literacyideas.com/teaching-cause-effect-in-english on October 7, 2022.

Mac Donnchaidh, S. (n.d.c). *Teaching compare and contrast.* Accessed at https://literacyideas.com/compare-and-contrast on December 30, 2022.

Mac Donnchaidh, S. (n.d.d). *What is an inference? And how to teach it.* Accessed at https://literacyideas.com/teaching-inference on December 26, 2022.

Macon, J. M., Bewell, D., & Vogt, M. E. (1991). *Responses to literature: Grades K–8.* Newark, DE: International Reading Association.

Maine Department of Education. (2020, July). *English language arts standards.* Augusta, ME: Author. Accessed at www.maine.gov/doe/learning/content/ela/standards on October 7, 2022.

Marye, S. (n.d.). How to teach Greek and Latin roots in upper elementary [Blog post]. *The Stellar Teacher Company.* Accessed at www.stellarteacher.com/blog/teaching-greek-and-latin-roots on December 22, 2022.

Marzano, R. J. (2010, April 1). *The art and science of teaching / Teaching inference.* Accessed at www.ascd.org/el/articles/teaching-inference-april-2010 on October 7, 2022.

Marzano, R. J., & Pickering, D. J. (2005). *Building academic vocabulary: Teacher's manual.* Alexandria, VA: ASCD.

Massachusetts Department of Elementary and Secondary Education. (2021, June 22). *Tiered instruction within the MTSS model.* Accessed at www.doe.mass.edu/massliteracy/leading-mtss/tiered-instruction.html on October 5, 2022.

Massachusetts Department of Elementary and Secondary Education. (2022, November 8). *Current frameworks.* Accessed at www.doe.mass.edu/frameworks/current.html on December 15, 2022.

MasterClass. (2021, August 23). *What is subtext? Learn the definition and role of subtext in writing, plus 5 tips to better incorporate subtext in your work.* Accessed at www.masterclass.com/articles/what-is-subtext-learn-the-definition-and-role-of-subtext-in-writing-plus-5-tips-to-better-incorporate-subtext-in-your-work on December 26, 2022.

McArdle, E. (2014, Fall). What happened to the Common Core? *Ed Magazine.* Accessed at www.gse.harvard.edu/news/ed/14/09/what-happened-common-core on October 6, 2022.

McKneely, M. (2020, April 9). *Common Core just mostly dead.* Accessed at https://hslda.org/post/common-core-just-mostly-dead on October 5, 2022.

Merritt, E. G. (2016, December 1). *Time for teacher learning, planning critical for school reform.* Accessed at https://kappanonline.org/time-teacher-learning-planning-critical-school-reform on October 7, 2022.

Montero, M. (2021, January 22). *The complete guide to teaching prefixes and suffixes.* Accessed at https://teachingwithamountainview.com/teaching-prefixes-and-suffixes/# on December 22, 2022.

Moore, C. (2017, March 7). *5 essential strategies to help students meet rigorous standards* [Blog post]. Accessed at www.learningsciences.com/blog/5-essential-strategies-to-help-students-meet-rigorous-standards on October 6, 2022.

Munch, E. (1893). *The scream* [Painting]. Oslo, Norway: National Museum. Accessed at www.edvardmunch.org/the-scream.jsp on January 26, 2023.

National Governors Association Center for Best Practices & Council of Chief State School Officers. (2010). *Common Core State Standards for English language arts and literacy in history/social studies, science, and technical subjects.* Washington, DC: Authors. Accessed at www.corestandards.org/assets/CCSSI_ELA%20Standards.pdf on October 7, 2022.

National Institute for Literacy. (2007). *What content-area teachers should know about adolescent literacy.* Washington, DC: Author. Accessed at https://lincs.ed.gov/publications/pdf/adolescent_literacy07.pdf on October 6, 2022.

National Society of High School Scholars. (2020, December 3). *5 benefits of collaborative learning strategies and how to get started* [Blog post]. Accessed at www.nshss.org/blog/5-benefits-of-collaborative-learning-strategies-how-to-get-started on December 14, 2022.

Newsela. (2016, August 12). *Racer blades: Do high-tech artificial limbs give athletes an edge?* Accessed at https://newsela.com/read/blade-runners-advantage/id/20483 on October 6, 2022.

Ng, B. (2018). The neuroscience of growth mindset and intrinsic motivation. *Brain Sciences, 8*(2), 20. Accessed at www.ncbi.nlm.nih.gov/pmc/articles/PMC5836039 on October 6, 2022.

Nietzel, M. T. (2020, September 9). Low literacy levels among U.S. adults could be costing the economy $2.2 trillion a year. *Forbes.* Accessed at www.forbes.com/sites/michaeltnietzel/2020/09/09/low-literacy-levels-among-us-adults-could-be-costing-the-economy-22-trillion-a-year on October 6, 2022.

O'Mahony, K. (2021). *The brain-based classroom: Accessing every child's potential through educational neuroscience.* New York: Routledge.

Odell Education. (2020, August). *Building evidenced-based arguments: Developing core proficiencies English language arts / literacy unit, grade 11*. Portland, ME: Author. Accessed at www.odelleducation.com/wp-content/uploads/2020/08/Argumentation-Unit-Plan-G11.pdf on January 1, 2023.

Parekh, N., Ali, S. H., O'Connor, J., Tozan, Y., Jones, A. M., Capasso, A., et al. (2021). Food insecurity among households with children during the COVID-19 pandemic: Results from a study among social media users across the United States. *Nutrition Journal, 20*(1), 73. https://doi.org/10.1186/s12937-021-00732-2

Parrish, N. (2022, May 23). *Teaching students to assess their learning*. Accessed at www.edutopia.org/article/teaching-students-assess-their-learning on October 6, 2022.

PBS LearningMedia. (2013). *Comparing and contrasting information and forming an opinion: Santiago and Morris*. Accessed at https://wisconsin.pbslearningmedia.org/resource/vtl07.la.ws.research.lpformop/comparing-and-contrasting-information-and-forming-an-opinion-santiago-and-morris on January 3, 2023.

Pennsylvania Training and Technical Assistance Network. (2019). *Effective practices for teaching academic vocabulary*. Accessed at https://bit.ly/3kx0Ozh on December 22, 2022.

Plaisance, P. L. (2020, December 16). Relying on social media for your news? Not a good idea [Blog post]. *Psychology Today*. Accessed at www.psychologytoday.com/us/blog/virtue-in-the-media-world/202012/relying-social-media-your-news-not-good-idea on January 1, 2023.

Poe, E. A. (2021, July 3). *The cask of Amontillado*. Accessed at https://poemuseum.org/the-cask-of-amontillado on October 6, 2022. (Original work published 1846)

Poorvu Center for Teaching and Learning. (n.d.). *Transfer of knowledge to new contexts*. Accessed at https://poorvucenter.yale.edu/TransferKnowledge on October 6, 2022.

Project Play Therapy. (2021, June 24). *Compare and contrast activity page*. Accessed at www.projectplaytherapy.com/compare-and-contrast-activity-page on December 30, 2022.

Queensland Brain Institute. (n.d.). *How are memories formed?* Accessed at https://qbi.uq.edu.au/brain-basics/memory/how-are-memories-formed on February 16, 2022.

Read Naturally. (n.d.). *Sketching vocabulary words: Valuable word-learning strategy*. Accessed at www.readnaturally.com/article/sketching-vocabulary-words-valuable-word-learning-strategy on December 25, 2022.

Reading Rockets. (n.d.a). *Self-esteem*. Accessed at www.readingrockets.org/helping/self-esteem on October 6, 2022.

Reading Rockets. (n.d.b). *Summarizing*. Accessed at www.readingrockets.org/strategies/summarizing on December 20, 2022.

Recht, D. R., & Leslie, L. (1988). Effect of prior knowledge on good and poor readers' memory of text. *Journal of Educational Psychology, 80*(1), 16–20. https://doi.org/10.1037/0022-0663.80.1.16

Red Nose Day. (2019, November 1). *Changing illiteracy in the U.S. with early initiatives*. Accessed at https://rednoseday.org/news/changing-illiteracy-and-poverty-in-america on October 6, 2022.

Redden, A. (2015, June 12). *The importance of rigor in any standards*. Accessed at www.ednc.org/the-importance-of-rigor-in-any-standards on October 6, 2022.

Reg Erhardt Library. (2022, November 21). *RADAR for evaluating information: RADAR*. Accessed at https://libguides.sait.ca/RADAR on January 26, 2023.

Rigor. (n.d.). In *Dictionary.com*. Accessed at www.dictionary.com/browse/rigor on October 7, 2022.

Roell, K. (2019a, July 3). *How to find the main idea*. Accessed at www.thoughtco.com/how-to-find-the-main-idea-3212047 on October 6, 2022.

Roell, K. (2019b, August 19). *Inference: A critical assumption.* Accessed at www.thoughtco.com/what-is-an-inference-3211727 on December 26, 2022.

Rogers, K. (2019, October 29). *US teens use screens more than seven hours a day on average—and that's not including school work.* Accessed at www.cnn.com/2019/10/29/health/common-sense-kids-media-use-report-wellness/index.html on January 2, 2023.

RTI Action Network. (n.d.). *What is RTI?* Accessed at www.rtinetwork.org/learn/what/whatisrti on October 5, 2022.

Saunders, E. (2023). *Stick the learning: Brain-based teaching techniques to increase retention, application, and transfer.* Bloomington, IN: Solution Tree Press.

Schlechty, P. C. (2011). *Engaging students: The next level of working on the work.* San Francisco: Jossey-Bass.

Schmidt, M., Egger, F., Benzing, V., Jäger, K., Conzelmann, A., Roebers, C. M., et al. (2017). Disentangling the relationship between children's motor ability, executive function and academic achievement. *PLoS One, 12*(8), e0182845.

Schmidt, M., Jäger, K., Egger, F., Roebers, C. M., & Conzelmann, A. (2015). Cognitively engaging chronic physical activity, but not aerobic exercise, affects executive functions in primary school children: A group-randomized controlled trial. *Journal of Sport and Exercise Psychology, 37*(6), 575–591.

Shakespeare, W. (2004). *Romeo and Juliet* (B. A. Mowat & P. Werstine, Eds.; annotated ed.). New York: Simon & Schuster. (Original work published 1597)

Shanahan, T. (2020, March 14). *Prior knowledge, or he isn't going to pick on the baseball study* [Blog post]. Accessed at www.shanahanonliteracy.com/blog/prior-knowledge-or-he-isnt-going-to-pick-on-the-baseball-study on October 6, 2022.

Shapiro, E. S. (n.d.). *Tiered instruction and intervention in a response-to-intervention model.* Accessed at www.rtinetwork.org/essential/tieredinstruction/tiered-instruction-and-intervention-rti-model on October 5, 2022.

Smekens Education Solutions. (2017a, April 15). *Add 6 types of supporting details.* Accessed at www.smekenseducation.com/add-6-types-of-supporting-details on December 19, 2022.

Smekens Education Solutions. (2017b, January 17). *Follow 5 steps to make an inference.* Accessed at www.smekenseducation.com/follow-5-steps-to-make-an-inference on December 26, 2022.

Sparks, S. D. (2022, February 16). *More than 1 in 3 children who started school in the pandemic need "intensive" reading help.* Accessed at www.edweek.org/teaching-learning/more-than-1-in-3-children-who-started-school-in-the-pandemic-need-intensive-reading-help/2022/02 on October 7, 2022.

Srikrishna, R. (2021, February 8). *Food insecurity and COVID-19: The fight to feed America.* Accessed at www.teenvogue.com/story/food-insecurity-covid-united-states on December 14, 2022.

Stanford Graduate School of Education. (2021, May 27). *National study of high school students' digital skills paints worrying portrait, Stanford researchers say.* Accessed at https://ed.stanford.edu/news/national-study-high-school-students-digital-skills-paints-worrying-portrait-stanford on January 2, 2023.

Stobaugh, R. (2023). *30+ movement strategies to boost cognitive engagement: Activating minds and bodies to maximize student learning.* Bloomington, IN: Solution Tree Press.

Strickland, D. S., & Alvermann, D. E. (2004). Learning and teaching literacy in grades 4–12: Issues and challenges. In D. S. Strickland & D. E. Alvermann (Eds.), *Bridging the literacy achievement gap, grades 4–12* (pp. 1–13). New York: Teachers College Press.

Student Achievement Partners. (2021). *Foundational reading skills are, well, the foundation*. New York: Achieve the Core. Accessed at https://achievethecore.org/content/upload/4_Foundational%20 Skills.pdf on October 6, 2022.

StudySmarter. (n.d.). *Main idea and supporting detail*. Accessed at www.studysmarter.us/explanations /english/single-paragraph-essay/main-idea-and-supporting-detail on December 19, 2022.

Subtext. (n.d.). In *Dictionary.com*. Accessed at www.dictionary.com/browse/subtext on December 26, 2022.

Sunkara, V. K. M. (2019, Summer). *A data driven approach to identify journalistic 5Ws from text documents* [Master's thesis, University of Nebraska–Lincoln]. Computer Science and Engineering: Theses, Dissertations, and Student Research. https://digitalcommons.unl.edu/computerscidiss/172

Swan, M. (2019, December 12). *How important is teaching literacy in all content areas?* [Blog post]. Accessed at www.classcraft.com/blog/how-important-is-teaching-literacy-in-all-content-areas on October 5, 2022.

TeacherVision. (2019, November 15). *Cause and effect lesson*. Accessed at www.teachervision.com /professional-development/cause-effect-lesson on December 27, 2022.

Terada, Y. (2019, March 14). *The science of drawing and memory*. Accessed at www.edutopia.org/article /science-drawing-and-memory on December 25, 2022.

Terada, Y. (2022, August 5). *5 indispensable ways to deepen student comprehension*. Accessed at www .edutopia.org/article/5-indispensable-ways-deepen-student-comprehension on December 20, 2022.

Tomlinson, C. A., & Sousa, D. A. (2020, May 1). *The sciences of teaching*. Accessed at www.ascd.org/el /articles/the-sciences-of-teaching on October 6, 2022.

United Nations Children's Fund. (2022, March). *Are children really learning? Exploring foundational skills in the midst of a learning crisis*. New York: Author. Accessed at https://data.unicef.org/resources/are -children-really-learning-foundational-skills-report on November 8, 2022.

University of Kansas School of Education and Human Sciences. (n.d.). *Teaching literacy in your K–12 classrooms*. Accessed at https://educationonline.ku.edu/community/teaching-reading-and-writing -skills on October 7, 2022.

University of Wisconsin–Milwaukee. (2022). *Curriculum and instruction (CURRINS)*. Accessed at https:// catalog.uwm.edu/courses/currins/currins.pdf on January 2, 2023.

Weinberg, A. (2022, January 21). *Teaching students to evaluate websites*. Accessed at www.edutopia.org /article/teaching-students-evaluate-websites on January 2, 2023.

Wenk, L. (2017, September 14). *The importance of engaging prior knowledge*. Accessed at https://sites .hampshire.edu/ctl/2017/09/14/the-importance-of-engaging-prior-knowledge on December 15, 2022.

Westman, L. (2021, September 1). *What differentiated instruction really means*. Accessed at www.ascd.org /el/articles/what-differentiated-instruction-really-means on October 6, 2022.

White, M. G. (2021, June 4). What are supporting details? *YourDictionary*. Accessed at https://grammar .yourdictionary.com/writing/what-are-supporting-details.html on December 19, 2022.

Wierman, M. (2021, January 15). *5 brain-based learning strategies to boost learning, retention, and focus* [Blog post]. Accessed at https://blog.edmentum.com/5-brain-based-learning-strategies-boost -learning-retention-and-focus on October 6, 2022.

Will, M. (2022, January 4). *What teachers can do to help struggling readers who feel ashamed*. Accessed at www.edweek.org/teaching-learning/what-teachers-can-do-to-help-struggling-readers-who-feel -ashamed/2022/01 on October 6, 2022.

William H. Hannon Library. (2020). *RADAR: Evaluating information sources for novice researchers.* Accessed at https://libguides.lmu.edu/ld.php?content_id=59083488 on December 31, 2022.

Wisconsin Department of Public Instruction. (n.d.a). *Academic standards.* Accessed at https://dpi.wi.gov/standards on October 6, 2022.

Wisconsin Department of Public Instruction. (n.d.b). *Family and consumer sciences education.* Accessed at https://dpi.wi.gov/fcs on October 6, 2022.

Wojcicki, E. (2021, October 8). *Teaching fact vs. opinion: Tips, activities, and resources* [Blog post]. Accessed at www.hmhco.com/blog/teaching-fact-versus-opinion on January 2, 2023.

Wyoming Department of Education. (n.d.). *Content and performance standards.* Accessed at https://edu.wyoming.gov/for-district-leadership/standards on December 15, 2022.

Yup. (2021, October 21). *The importance of building on students' prior knowledge* [Blog post]. Accessed at https://yup.com/blog/importance-building-on-prior-knowledge on December 15, 2022.

Zimmermann, F., Schütte, K., Taskinen, P., & Köller, O. (2013). Reciprocal effects between adolescent externalizing problems and measures of achievement. *Journal of Educational Psychology, 105*(3), 747–761. https://doi.org/10.1037/a0032793

Zolkoski, S. M. (2019). The importance of teacher-student relationships for students with emotional and behavioral disorders. *Preventing School Failure: Alternative Education for Children and Youth, 63*(3), 236–241.

INDEX

NUMBERS

A

B

C

D

E

F

G

H

I

J

K

L

M

N

O

P

R

S

Ready to Learn
Peg Grafwallner
Ready to Learn introduces the FRAME model, a teacher-approved approach for creating meaningful and motivating learning experiences for all students. Rely on the model's five steps to help you launch engaging lessons, articulate clear expectations, and offer effective feedback.
BKF922

Not Yet . . . And That's OK
Peg Grafwallner
Every learning challenge is an empowering opportunity to grow. With this teacher-friendly resource, you will learn how to help your students celebrate the academic experience, embrace productive struggle, and deeply value themselves as learners and risk takers.
BKG008

Literacy Reframed
Robin J. Fogarty, Gene M. Kerns, and Brian M. Pete
Discover a game-changing new way to think about—and teach—literacy at all levels. With *Literacy Reframed*, you will discover a dynamic path forward for creating classrooms that fully support students on their literacy journeys and prepare them to become lifelong lovers of reading.
BKF959

The Literacy Triangle
LeAnn Nickelsen and Melissa Dickson
Accelerate learning with high-impact strategies. Beginning and veteran teachers alike will find insights and practices they can use immediately. No matter what content area you teach, this book will help you develop the strategic reader in every student.
BKF983

Solution Tree | Press 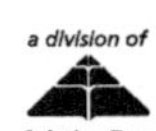

Visit SolutionTree.com or call 800.733.6786 to order.